DReaMS
FoR OuR
DauGHTeRS

A collection of dreams, wishes and perspectives for our collective daughters

BONNIE ALLMON COFFEY

ISBN: 1-886225-88-5

Library of Congress Control Number: 2002105338

Cover photo by Rob Wilken

Cover art by Liz Shea-McCoy
Cover design by Angie Johnson

DAGEFORDE
Publishing. inc.

Dageforde Publishing, Inc.
128 East 13th Street
Crete, Nebraska 68333
www.dageforde.com

Printed in the United States of America
10 9 8 7 6 5 4 3 2 1

For Mother, because I am hers...
For Jenny, because she is mine...
And for Michael...just because he is.

Nothing happens unless first a dream.
　　　　　—Carl Sandburg

Foreword

reams articulated become possibilities. The genius of Bonnie Coffey's book is that by giving women a voice for their dreams, she helps us take the first steps toward making those dreams come true. Say it out loud and a dream takes on shape and form and concrete possibility. Share it with others and give birth to a new reality.

The dreams offered up in this book, like offerings to the Goddess, constitute a collective vision of a world in which girls are welcome, safe, cherished, strong, and beloved. In this new world girls are not at risk for their physical safety, they are not beaten and not beaten down. Their voices ring loud and clear. They lead, make history, flex their muscles and exercise their voice—routinely.

In fact, part of what is so appealing about the dreams is the democratic nature of the new world women yearn for—these are not dreams of privilege or individual advantage. Instead, the visions are of a world in which justice and opportunity abound for all. It seems understood that such a world is a better world for all of us—not just for the daughters, granddaughters, nieces and goddaughters for whom we wish specific success, personal well being. Clearly, women seem to say with their dreams, as for my daughters—real and figurative—to be happy, secure, actualized, ALL girls (indeed all humans) must be happy, secure, actualized. This is an ambitious, bold, even grandiose, dream—and it reflects the courage of the women who contributed to the book.

Dreams for Our Daughters is a song of hope and joy. But it is also a subtext of grief, a collection of narratives that tell as much about dreams unrealized as possibilities imagined for the next generation.

What might our own lives have been—indeed how might the planet feel—if the dreams detailed for daughters were the realities of mothers' and grandmothers' and aunts' lives? While painting pictures of how the future SHOULD be, this book offers a quiet nod of admiration to the women who survived and triumphed in a world not yet girl friendly, not yet entirely safe for women, not yet universally welcoming to the female gender.

Like a reverent treasure hunter, Ms. Coffey has not just collected dreams but displayed them like jewels in a fine museum. This is a book to savor, revisit, ponder, and add to. Consider it a blueprint as well as a narrative. Experiment with envisioning dreams of your own. Imagine now making these dreams reality.

Joline Godfrey
CEO, Independent Means, Inc.

Acknowledgments

Heartfelt thanks and hugs and kisses to those many people who gave support, advice and help: to Linda Dageforde, who patiently waited until it was time; to Liz Shea-McCoy, whose unique and formidable talent matches her loving heart; to my mother, who nurtured my creative spirit and kept it alive when it was in danger of dying; to my daughter Jenny for her unconditional love and belief that I would, someday, get it all right; and to my partner in life, Michael, who catches my errors, fixes my spelling, is my biggest fan club member and loves me in spite of it all.

Introduction

The title for this book, *Dreams for Our Daughters*, was born of a real life dream. I don't know where it came from, I only know that once it was embedded in my creative mental file, it wouldn't budge. There it sat and grew and grew, finding form and substance until it finally pushed itself into existence—rather like giving birth. The message was to give women an opportunity to share their innermost dreams for our daughters—for their own, if they had daughters, or for our collective daughters as a whole. Even women who have sons have dreams for our daughters. Over the course of two years, the idea was honed and tweaked, and countless letters went out to women of all kinds of diverse backgrounds. There were periods of doubt and depression as requests for dreams went either unanswered or declined. The dream, however, persisted, and gained momentum. Dreams began coming in from both expected and unexpected sources...and each one was a treasure. Women shared stories and perspectives that humbled and amazed me. E-mails tumbled across the net, full of encouragement and support and thanks. Women in not only the United States, but across the seas sent in pieces of themselves in these writings.

What began as a lovely little idea turned into one of the most amazing journeys I've ever had.

These dreams and observations are from women whose names you will recognize, and from many whose names you will see for the first time. The dreams are from famous women, professional women, women incarcerated in prisons, rural women, stay-at-home moms and women who have lost their daughters. The dreams are from women who have daughters, women who have no daughters, and even women who have no children at all. The dreams are from women all over the world.

Share this book—with a young woman you know—to give her hope, perhaps some guidance, and certainly some inspiration. She, too, someday, will have *Dreams for Our Daughters.*

Bonnie Allmon Coffey

My dream for my daughter is much simpler than four pages! I just hope if she chooses to have a career outside her home or if she chooses to stay at home and raise children, she has a supportive world, community and nation to be a success. If she chooses to do both, I hope we have policies in place to allow her to do both well.

Patty Murray

Patty Murray is a United States Senator for the state of Washington.

The question asks, "what do I dream for my daughter and her future?" Oh, that's easy I want…It's not easy at all. Health, wealth and happiness? No, that is too casual a phrase. What I want for my daughter is so much more, but how do I describe it? How do you put into words that which only comes from the inner feeling that has grown from the moment of her conception? A very precious gift, so unique, so beautiful, that she outshines the rarest of jewels.

Obviously I want the very best for her. I want her to be what *she* wants to be, to realize *her* dreams, and if I can be there to help her, guide and support her, perhaps I will be fulfilling one of my dreams. I want for her to have the opportunities I never had, to learn from my mistakes. I want her to find true friendship and true love.

But what of the world she will be living in? I want for her to see its beauty and appreciate the endless number of wonderful creatures and places that it holds. I want for her to care for it, fight for it and protect it so that her children and her grandchildren, will also know its wonders. I wish her a world of peace, where Man has learned to live in harmony with the Earth and all that coexist here, whether it be plant, creature or fellow Man. I want her to remember my teachings in that true happiness is not found in material wealth but in the beauty of the flower, bird song, dew on a spider's web, dolphins playing—the richness of nature—for this is what would be missed the most if it were not there.

I know I will not always be beside her, and that she will eventually have to find her way through life, but I want her to know that if she ever needs it there will always be a path home. Hopefully, at the end of a long and happy life she will be able to look back and say "that was a good life," but most of all I hope she will say "my Mother was always my friend."

Christine P. Dodwell

Christine lives in northwest Scotland where she holds her daughter's hand with love and friendship.

I would wish that my daughter has a clearer vision of her roles than I did, both as an individual and as a woman. Like many women of my generation, I've wanted a career, and a home with children, and those two roles are hard to balance. I hope that our daughters will use their time wisely and responsibly, developing enough strength of character so that when career has to take second place to family, they can accept that responsibility with grace and pride. In the same way, I hope our daughters have the strength of character to distinguish which of their own children's demands are necessary and just, and which are not, and thereby mother with grace and wisdom.

May they have clarity of mind for wise decisions, self-esteem for confident decisions, and humility for selfless decisions.

Pippa White

Pippa does some of the most remarkable creative work I've seen. A performer of one-woman shows, Pippa is working on a depiction of a suffragette. Her work is seen across the country.

A Mother's Final Blessing

As you venture courageously into the world, I am dazzled by your poise and grace, and I am pierced with the regrets
of unfulfilled intentions,
unspoken words...
And words that intruded our symphony...
words that I wish I had never uttered...

It's easy, at a time like this,

to believe that I have failed miserably
at this thing called Motherhood.
I gave you life...
for better and for worse.
I did my best...
Hoping in my heart that you'd survive my
mistakes.

Dear Daughter of my soul,
you once inhabited my own flesh.
Indulge me this final Mother's plea
that I might right the wrongs
of my inexperience and immaturity.
Permit me this occasion to tell you
about the things that I have learned...
from you...
as we grew up together.

This I now know...

You are a gift.
You are beautiful and talented.
You deserve to be cherished and nurtured
and loved unconditionally...
for you are created in God's image.
In you resides the very same creative power
that formed the Universe...
for you are Woman...

compassionate, merciful, wise, patient, kind...
and strong.
The world may call you weak
but hold onto this enduring truth.
And know that you can trust your soul,
for it remembers the things
that your heart long ago forgot...
I gave you life...

but in truth...it was you who gave me life!
It was you who helped me to remember.
You taught me to sing...and to dance.
You gave me hope...and a future.
And so...the legacy of Woman goes on
as it has from generation to generation.
You carry the seed of the Divine...
the promise of greatness!

The world is waiting.
Go...
I love you.
Kathy Hurt

A creative, spiritual soul, Kathy is a musician and artist in Virginia whose CD, "Coming Home," is available at www.indieheaven.com.

I have dreams for my daughters, Debra and Darcie, and for Donna, my daughter-in-law gained through our son Dean's marriage. My dream extends to all daughters and for those touched by all of our dreams.

I have been a lifelong learner. I wish for my daughters to experience the joy of learning throughout their lives. I hope that their love of learning will propel them to continue to grow in wisdom—and to become their best selves. One of my favorite quotes encourages us to do just that. "Today, sculpt and work on your life. You are creating a masterpiece. Everyone is an artist in partnership with their Creator." Each new experience in my life has taught me something. Children have taught me to be honest and open, to share freely, and to be myself.

Someone once said, "There are two kinds of people in the world—the givers and the takers." I suppose that all of us *give* some and *take* some. It's probably true that there is a time to give and a time to take. I hope that my daughters will share their time and energy to give a "lift" to others along their life paths. "Lifting" gives us a boost. At the same time, we enrich another person's life.

One of my personal reminders states, "Do what you can do. Don't worry about what you can't do. Pray for guidance to discern what you can and can't do."

As the saying goes, "Just do it!" It's easy to spin our wheels trying to decide what needs to be done. Instead, we can find one way to jump in and make a positive impact. It's easy to complain, "The world today is so violent." It takes time and energy to listen to an angry child or an angry adult and make a difference in their life. There are so many ways of lifting—listening, sharing our talents and our resources, and offering words of encourage-ment. Each of us can lift in our own unique way.

A valuable dream for my daughters envisions that they love life—all of life—with its ups and downs. I want an eagerness to spread that love of life to others through genuine caring and respect for all persons. I wish enjoyment of *each* day, brightened with a touch of humor and fun. That love of life is undergirded with a spirit of opti-mism. A favorite quote says it well: "Optimism—a cheerful frame of mind that enables a teakettle to sing, though in hot water up to its nose." That kind of "can do" spirit refuses to succumb to despair in any circumstance. That "love of life" spirit looks for ways to share God's love each day.

I dream that my daughters will live their lives to keep alive a legacy of learning, lifting and loving passed on by my mother and grandmothers. It's easy to say, "I don't have time." It's harder to *make* time for dreaming and doing—for learning, lifting and loving.

As a lover of butterflies, I'll close with this prayerful thought. "The butterfly counts not months, but moments, and yet has time enough. Time—oh, Lord, how swiftly it seems to fly. Thank you for reminding me that there is time enough for what You have planned for my life."

Lois Poppe

Part of her "lifting" is teaching immigrant and refugee women English and being active in the League of Women Voters.

essica, as you know, it is my desire that we all operate on an equal playing field so that our successes are achieved, rather than ascribed by virtue of position. I have found that usually those who achieve success are also those who want to give (to their friends, community, nation) more than they get, just because it is the right thing to do. These are also the people who act with integrity, because their word costs nothing to give, but it may be the hardest thing to keep. It is my dream that this will be your world. A world of equality, in which we will all treat each other with dignity and respect.

Nancy Intermill

A dear friend, Nancy is active in Business and Professional Women and has served as a state president. She is a strong advocate for women's rights.

I would want my daughter to know that I believe there are only joys and lessons in life, not joys and sorrows. Viewing any of our experiences as sorrows results in resisting the reality, hoping to change the experience, to avert or divert. Accepting the non-joys as lessons is the better alternative. If you learn something from the experience, that was its lesson for you. If the experience makes you better or stronger, that was its meaning. But, there are only joys and lessons.

I would want my daughter to know that God/the Universe is highly more benevolent than malevolent.

I would want my daughter to know that the 10 Commandments are 10 very good suggestions. And that we will not be asked at the end of Life how many times we did or didn't violate them, but rather whether we had a good time and whether anyone else had to pay dues for our good time.

Peg Armstrong

Peg is a psychotherapist who has known my family for over thirty-five years. She is a guiding spirit that encourages growth and self-discovery. Still practicing, she owns and operates an ashram.

have a son, so my dream for our "daughters" must also include my son. The dream is much the same for both. As an African American, my dream is that education be used to provide the path to your success. Education in truly the broadest sense of the word. Knowledge that boosts your self esteem, love and curiosity for life. Education that allows you to choose your path in life.

Caroline R. Jones

President and CEO of Caroline Jones Advertising, Inc., Ms. Jones heads an African-American owned ad agency and is the first Black female vice president of a major advertising agency.

believe that our dreams for our children never stop, but do change as our children grow to become who they are in life. I believe that we all want more for our children than we had in life. We wish for lifelong happiness for our children. The hard part is to know what happiness for them looks like, versus what happiness to us looks like. The one dream I have is that all children could enjoy a happy, fulfilled life.

DREAMS FOR OUR DAUGHTERS

When I was pregnant, I began thinking of "the perfect family" dreams that would include a daughter. Those dreams included that she would be beautiful, more talented, better educated, have a better job, and of course, more independent than me. I dreamed of a child who was kind hearted and a Christian who would someday be a wife and mother herself. I dreamed of generations of women in our family doing family holidays in the kitchen, shopping and enjoying generations of new babies.

Jennifer was beautiful inside and out, so my dreams grew toward hoping she would attend college and have a career that would guarantee her financial independence. I began to dream that it would be important for her to have talents that would be used in life skills, so that she could be independent. Once again, dreams came true. Her independence and athletic abilities surprised all of us. She was now beautiful, a good athlete, wonderful with children she baby-sat and at the daycare, as well as independent. Along with those attributes, she was a Christian who insisted on including her friends in church activities—especially Sunday school. I realized that my dreams for her had begun to come true. The only dream left was that she go to college, and enjoy a family life and career.

Then in one moment we lost her, and then I only dreamed of how wonderful it would be to just have her here with me. You see, all those visions we have for our daughters are not as important as just having the opportunity to hug them one more time. So my dream now is just to see her again and that will happen someday—when we meet in Heaven.

For daughters everywhere, in all walks of life, I wish for you profound happiness. Only you can know what that looks like for you. Happiness comes in different packages; for some it's wrapped with families, friends and children while for others its wrapped in careers. Find your own personal happiness and enjoy it—this is my dream for you.

Pamela Bratton

Pam was a mentor of mine many years ago, tucking me under her very experienced wing and helping me along the way. She introduced me to American Business Women's Association, where she has served on the national level. She is in the human resources business and is one very savvy professional.

In trying to write this essay for *Dreams for Our Daughters*, I found that I had trouble. Not that I didn't have dreams for my daughter; on the contrary, I have LOTS of dreams for my daughter. But how could I isolate just one or two? How could I separate the dreams I have for my child from the dreams I have for all children, for all of humanity's daughters and sons? And what is the difference between hopes and dreams? Can dreams come true or, by their very nature, are dreams ephemeral and so big that we have to classify them in some category that comes only when we enter an alternative consciousness like sleep?

Phew, I said to myself, Karen, stop resisting. Dreams for our daughters...this seems straightforward enough. Stop overanalyzing. Edit this at will, Bonnie!

First, I have to admit that I wanted a daughter. My daughter is my first child, and I wanted a girl. I know that you are not supposed to say that, just say you want a healthy child, but darned if I didn't want a healthy baby girl. I wanted a daughter to dream for so much that I didn't dare to dream for one, I just assumed I'd be having a boy! And when I found out it was a girl, I was absolutely and truly delighted. A daughter! Just what I wanted!

Why did I want a daughter so badly? At the time, I only knew that I wished for a girl child; now, having lived with her for ten years, I believe that I wanted a girl because I daily strive to make a world wherein girls can do anything, and I wanted her to be one of the first to be able to reach the stars! Even though I personally have reaped the benefits of the women's movement by coming of age in the 1970s, I am acutely aware at all times that things are still not fair for women and girls. Beyond salaries and health issues, the basic fact is that the world is not as open and welcoming to women as it is to men. In fact, we live in a world that is downright dangerous for women, both in overt and subtle ways. Case in point: yesterday, October 27, 1999, I had a telephone conversation with a young man who is directing a play called the *Fantasticks*. If you are not familiar with this piece, don't bother rushing out to read or see it; despite its big claim to fame (it is the longest running Off-Broadway play), it is a musical about nothing much, a good-time musical. Now, I have nothing against a good time, but I do when it oppresses someone. And this play does, subtly, with its words: a song in the play celebrates and plans a joyous event for the daughter of a main character—the rape of that daughter. The play is over 40 years old, and the song doesn't mean rape as we think of it today; still, the word is there, sung over and over again. Four years ago, while I fought to have this song eliminated from a production at the theater where I worked, I discovered that I was not the only one offended by the song. The playwrights had, in response to the changing times, written another version of the song (minus the word rape) which my theater used in its production. Anyway, during my conversation with this young man, I laughingly said that I hoped that he was using the non-rape song and he replied, well there are two definitions of rape in the dictionary, and besides the rape song was the better song. I was baffled and speechless—he didn't get it? And I was too astounded to explain it coherently and ended up babbling on about my daughter, how I wouldn't take my daughter to this play, any play that celebrates "rape," no matter what you mean, because of what it means. He still didn't *get it*, I fear I offended him, and I kicked myself for my lack of eloquence. Dream #1: I dream a world where violence against women will be a thing of the past, where everyone will get it, where a woman will not be raped every few seconds, and where men will not mix up sex and violence, even semantically. Ever. And I dream this world for my daughter. NOW. Am I dreaming yet?

Sigh. The sad fact is that we still have so much to dream for our daughters (and, if we are honest, for our sons as well). Dreams of equality do not play biological favorites. Dreams of peaceful coexistence with one another, dreams of love and happiness, are not sex or gender biased. I dream of love and happiness for my daughter and my son. I want them to have opportunities to realize happiness, all opportunities, and I want them to be able to experience love in whatever form they may wish. I feel like Martin Luther King, Jr., dreaming of a world where people are judged by the content of their character, not the color of their skin—or what is between their legs. These dreams take on specific significance when I think of my daughter: what opportunities will be denied her because she is my daughter and not my son? How will this affect her happiness? So I dream that no one will get in the way, knowingly or unknow-ingly, of her dreams. I dream that my daughter won't get raped. I dream that she will not get trapped in "the beauty myth," but I know that unless we move into the woods, far from other people, she probably will. I dream that she will never doubt her body or its abilities to do what she wants it to do. I dream that she will never hate men because of what they have done to her, or to her foremothers. I dream that she will be fair and loving and strong.

And because I dream so resolutely, I do things that embarrass my daughter! I talk to the PE teacher about the posters in the gym—the ones of famous sports figures, all men. I ask my co-worker who got married why she changed her name (she didn't know, but I asked anyway). I sport bumper stickers that say, "Feminism is the radical notion that women are people," and "Another family against Hate." I don't shave my underarms. I don't wear make-up. And I make art that strives for social justice as well as aesthetics.

We thought long and hard about what to name our daughter, our first born child. We decided to put our dreams into words, to give our daughter a name that would be hers alone, because she is who she is. We resisted the patriarchal imperative of giving a child the father's surname; instead, we dreamed up one for her, based on our two names. I am Karen Libman; my partner is Mitch Kachun, our daughter would be—a Kachman. We were and still are delighted by her name, which we also gave to her sibling. It means so much to me to have done this. You cannot believe the reactions to this name. I've had people (men) actually argue with me about it, telling me that I am paranoid and over sensitive, that their mothers were independent women and still had their father's names, that children need to know where they came from, and what family name would she carry? Ah, I would reply, she carries her family in her name—and in her person; her heritage lies in her heart, not in her daddy. Her name represents the shedding of patriarchal tradition, it represents to me that she can, indeed, do anything, dream anything, she is prepared, she knows where she has come from—and where she is going.

I dream this for me. And I dream this for my only daughter, Michelle Kari Kachman. So may it be.

Karen Libman

Karen is a creative spirit that infuses her work with her feminist philosophies, including a piece on the impact of pornography on our society.

I dream that our daughters will grow up in a safe environment, in a society that cherishes them for who they are, and that offers them equal opportunity in education and career choices.

This utopia will accept and respect those women who choose to be stay-at-home mothers and those who choose to combine parenting with a career. Moms working outside the home will have quality, affordable daycare. Women will support and honor each other's choices; women will not be pitted against women.

I dream that our daughters will be taught in elementary school about the struggles of our women ancestors, they who fought so valiantly for abolition of slavery and for the right to vote, for peace, dignity and freedom for all people. Our daughters will appreciate and learn from those women who have gone before so that they understand the importance of continuing the fight for that still-elusive goal—full equality under the law.

And finally, I dream that each of our daughters will have one lifelong friend with whom to share secrets, joys and sorrows, successes and disappointments, but most of all with whom to laugh...and soar to new heights.

Phyllis Bratt

Phyllis shares my love of stamps that feature women, honoring their history and gifts.

y dreams for my daughters, grand-daughter and all women—

- That you can maintain your independence and develop a solid feeling of self-worth.

- Find satisfaction and contentment in your personal lives and in whatever career or careers you pursue.

- Have a life that is rich and rewarding, filled with love of family and friends, combined with compassion and tolerance for others.

- That you never cease to learn, maintain a wide range of interests, and remain open to new experiences and risks.

- That you develop and maintain a good set of values in making judgments and resist compromise that is inconsistent with your values.

- Identify the priorities that guide your actions and update them throughout life.

- Have the strength and judgment to cope objectively with problems as they occur.

- Always maintain a sense of humor, remembering that we pass through this life only once and that life is transitional.

- Remember that you are in charge of your own attitude, the only person you can control is yourself.

- Be a part of the changing "community" with an awareness of what is good, what needs changing and what you can contribute to make it better. Be involved.

- Count your blessings and remember those who helped you acquire them and the need to pass that help along.

Ina May Rouse

Ina May is a dear friend who taught me that friends can be of all ages. An active member of OWL—The Voice of Midlife and Older Women, Ina May has served on their national board and is a political guru. Into her 70s, Ina May continues to be a caretaker for her ninety-six-year-old mother.

My fondest wish for our daughters is that they are raised in homes that are loving and caring. I would hope that they are nurtured and encouraged from the time they are born until they leave home, and even after. If a child receives good values from loving parents, she will become an individual who is thoughtful, confident, and a true partner in her marriage, in her workplace, and in her community. For those daughters who become parents, I wish them healthy children and the patience, understanding and love to provide those children with happy memories of their childhood and a blueprint for the future.

DiAnna Schimek

A true supporter of women, DiAnna represents the 27th District of Nebraska in the state Unicameral. She is credited with penning the legislation that mandated statewide insurance coverage for mammograms.

ooking back twenty years ago, my wishes for young women would have been different. I would have told them to get their degree in business administration or computer science. But the world has changed and continues to change. I believe our mothers of yesteryears are going to become our daughters of the future.

Do not ever underestimate the power of a degree or as much education as you can afford. Take advantage of education no matter what your age. Whether you obtain a degree or not, take time to read, preferably in the areas of non-fiction, self-help, self reliance and new skills. One of the most educated women I ever met never obtained her college degree. She acquired her high school diploma in her late twenties and never left the farm where she was raised. She was very poor most of her life but she read. When she died, they removed from her home and donated over 35,000 books that she had read. That woman was my grandmother and she could talk to anyone about any subject in an educated manner.

Learn as many home skills as possible—cooking, cleaning, gardening of vegetables, farm skills, building skills (small or large), sewing, knitting, crocheting, the list is endless. Find those skills you enjoy and practice them. Not only will you discover many stress relieving hobbies, but if there arrives a day your degree and education fail you, you will survive! Cleaning may not be a glamourous job, but in a pinch or even on purpose, it'll put a roof over your head and food on the table.

Lastly, learn to be your own best friend and find pride in caring for yourself. There is no other man or woman who can or will take care of your emotional and spiritual needs as well as you can. It is acceptable to spoil yourself a bit in order for you to be happy (and this does not necessarily take money to do). Only when you are happy, can you in turn pass that happiness on to someone else.

Cheryl P. Snyder

Although Cheryl and I have never met face-to-face, we are kindred spirits. We became acquainted through an online auction site when I began purchasing first day covers with stamps that feature women. She has shared e-pictures of the goats she raises and assured me that they really are as adorable as they appear.

My mother had divine dreams for me...and I wish for all little girls what my mother hoped and dreamed for me.

First of all: she always respected my early signs of complete independence. She always encouraged my inner strength to accomplish whatever it was that I set out to do in life. She was full of courage and positive spirit and she certainly instilled these qualities of inner character into me. She gave the best advice and was always available to discuss and evaluate every situation that might need it. She encouraged conversation and openness between us and she was always my best friend. There was nothing we could not exchange between us. I never felt that she did not have my best interest at heart and she was always there for me. Therefore, she taught me about friendship and loyalty and devotion to those you love. It has served me well!

If it were not for my mother's guidance and support, I would never have been what I am today. She has made me understand how proud we should be of our achievements and our success and because of her, I was able to be free as an artist and a person and she encouraged me "to fly" and become whatever I wanted to be....

She dreamed only beautiful wishes for me...she gave me all her wisdom which was enormous at all times, never holding back...the truth, that was her main aim...always the truth... "from here we march forward," she would always say.

She dreamed for me that I would be secure, not in just money, but in my own skin, my own person. "Live your life with wisdom and for yourself, like you like yourself—have respect for yourself. Everything else that you deserve will follow."

Today, I am Brenda Vaccaro, my mother's daughter, filled with her dreams, wishes and wisdom, ready for my own daughter to carry on "our dreams" for her.

Brenda Vaccaro

Born in Brooklyn, Brenda Vaccaro grew up in Dallas, Texas. She has a distinguished career in stage, film and television—her debut was in Midnight Cowboy.

My dream for our daughters is that they live from the core of their being—from their inner spirit. By living life from this center they can truly feel empowered with their own strength, wisdom and beauty. This will anchor them to their personal "star."

Living from this center will give them validation of their own worth, freeing them from seeking this in the outside world. Sometimes cultures define roles and images for women that are not healthy or realistic. Yet women try to live up to those expectations, losing themselves in the process.

These artificial expectations set women up to receive their value from the outside world through how they look, behave and live. If cultural standards are not met, the value of a woman as a person is not appreciated. When this happens, women become afraid of not being loved, worthy or deserving; so they try even harder to live up to these artificial external expectations. Often this cycle of fear rules their lives.

So—my wish for our daughters is that they live from the essence of whom they are—from a sense that they are loved and lovable, worthy, and deserving. Living from this truth gives our daughters "power from within!"

Sue McDaniel

Sue headed the Missouri Women's Council for many years and now works on responsible welfare reform. She is the coauthor of "Learning, Changing, Leading: Keys to Success in the 21st Century," with Chet Dixon.

y dream for my daughter, Andrea, is that all *her* dreams come true!

Unselfishly, B. J. Dennis

Once a building manager, B.J. quit her job to pursue her dream of becoming a massage therapist. Today, she owns a country spa retreat.

To my daughters, my children, my friends—
Amy and Angie…

I'm first obligated to acknowledge my gratitude at being given the opportunity to participate in this book. In the overall scheme of things, only a few women will be able to participate. Thanks, Bonnie for asking!

Second of all, I want you to be sure to read the other messages being sent in this book. I know that there is a wealth of information, guidance and love to be gleaned from this special collection. We may not all be writers by trade, but the messages come from the heart.

Now to the heart of the matter for me—this book comes at an exciting time in our lives. Both of you are finding your way in the world as young women. College graduations, job resumes, cross country moves, a tapestry of relationships. Treasure each experience! If you will think back, some of our most hearty laughs have been brought by a story that one of you has experienced.

You both know that I am long on advice. I'm learning to try and modify when to give and when to stifle. This comes as a lesson for me at this time in my life. One thing is for sure, continue to learn and challenge yourselves. Learn about everything. There is so much out there and those individuals that continue to learn are players, not spectators.

Be patient, be kind and be forgiving. These are personal assets that we would should all strive to have. I think you'll find that as you get older, you'll wish that you had a little more of at least one of those characteristics.

Don't be afraid to take chances. Failure is only in not having tried at all. It should be noted that you don't need to beat yourself up over issues either. If it doesn't work out, so be it. Move on. Keep moving!

Work hard and be honest. How many times have I told you that what is important in judging a person is, do they work hard and are they honest? In my opinion, these are two characteristics that transcend age, race, economic status, and religion. Be honest and work hard and I'm guessing that many, many people will be proud to call you friend.

Have a strong faith. If you don't have it now, develop it. It will get you through most any situation. Try and chat with the Lord frequently. I'm guessing you'll get some of your best lessons from Him.

Finally, take care of your physical self. Cherish your health. I know that may be another difficult one to grasp the concept of, but I can't stress enough that hereditary factors should be evaluated and then lifestyle adjustments made to assure a long life. If you don't feel well, many things become a struggle. Consider your health one of your best friends and treat it accordingly. Don't consider that a doctor can repair everything.

Above all, know that I love each of you. You are both so different and yet so much alike. Thank you for allowing me and challenging me to be a good parent. I made mistakes along the way and yet, I think that you have forgiven those. I'm pleased that we are close and consider that to be my greatest success. I love you both.

Love, Mom
Sandy Johnson

Sandy is an enthusiastic supporter of girls and women in sports and fitness and has one of the most optimistic attitudes of anyone I know.

My dreams for my daughter are the unconditional love my grandmother had for me—that she will have for her daughter and the wisdom my grandmother gave me. I still remember my grandmother singing to me, "Amazing Grace," how sweet the sound that was to me. I could always find peace and serenity at my grandmother's house. No matter how difficult times were, my grandmother always accepted me at her door.

Remembering one time I went to my grandmother's, I had two black eyes, a busted ear drum and a broken jaw. My boyfriend had beaten me up. I had hitchhiked from Ohio to Kentucky to get there to her house. She took me in and prayed for me and took care of my wounds and healing of my soul.

I will always remember my grandmother with such great love and admiration and wisdom. I hope my daughter will instill in her daughter all that my grandmother was to me.

Marsha Diane Ortiz

Marsha is a grandmother of three and has a passion for cooking, with dreams of becoming a chef.

My first thoughts on the title, *Dreams for Our Daughters*, is that you cannot and should not expect to live your own dreams through your daughters. They have to have their own dreams and wishes.

My dreams for my daughter were for her not to have the previous life I had, and that she achieved her own dreams and wishes and would have a good education, meet people and travel as I had not done, and realize that not every man you meet is the same and the right person would be out there somewhere in years to come.

Everyone's life has a different path to follow and every one is an individual.

But most of all go for your dreams, first and foremost, if at all possible.

These words might not appear clear at first, but all will become apparent in the following passages.

My daughter Joanne was 25 years of age on the 10th of October 1999. She was as a small child very quiet, quite happy with a book or drawing pad, had a very bright and articulate imagination. The treat for the week was not a bag of sweeties but the latest ladybird edition. The biggest upheaval in her early senior school years was the divorce of her father and I, who unfortunately felt that women were second-class citizens and were only good enough for rearing children and making sure a hot meal was on the table; he was also a heavy drinker. This did not give Joanne a stable family life or a lot of encouragement. I tried to instill in her she was as good as any man and any goal set out was possible. By the time Joanne was in her final year in senior school, she had decided to work toward further study and wished to work as a translator.

But as this was not thought of as a chosen subject for a girl in 1989, she was put off by her career advisors at the time; thus, she turned to a sports studies course instead, enabling her to prove she was as good and better than any teenage young man in her group and went all out to prove with sheer determination and an over-zealousness she was "better than any man." Where had that quiet studious girl gone to? With the determination that would have suited the Royal Marines! I remarried in 1990 and my husband was then in the Royal Marines. Maybe this is where the over determination stemmed from!

Maybe I was a bit too strong on the "you can be as good as the next man!"—pardon the pun. After the completion of a one year sports studies course, Joanne still felt languages were her forté!

She then embarked on a course of levels in English, art and photography. Once she had achieved these she decided to apply for the University and entered Portsmouth University in 1994 earning a four year Degree in Russian and Soviet Studies. I hasten to add she spent a year out in Russia living in St. Petersburg and Moscow. This Joanne welcomed, as she had first embarked on travel from the age of 14 years by spending two weeks in Maryland in USA with the Sea Cadets.

With the degree completed she continued with a Masters in Russian Language and Society and is presently awaiting the results (October 1999).

So, all in all, dreams have been achieved with a definite determination that maybe has a little more edge than normal. But Joanne has turned out to be a well-adjusted, hard working young lady, who is not at all boastful and lacks confidence in her own achievements. Joanne still has quirky times of insecurity and lacking confidence but after taking a few steps back, is ready to start again. But will always go for what she feels is best for her at the end of the day, quietly and unassumingly.

I can say that most of the dreams for my daughter have been achieved.

Dianne Deirdre-Bailey

Working on her degree, Dianne lives in the green hills of Scotland.

If I had a dream for a daughter, it would be that she realize that there are no limitations on what she can do or be. I would want her to realize that people are people. It doesn't matter what age they are, what gender they are, what color they are. What matters is what is in their heads and their hearts. The outside is just wrapping paper, what matters most are the treasures inside. I would dream of a day when women don't purposely set themselves apart from men and men don't purposely set themselves apart from women. Rather, we respect each other for our ideas.

If I had a dream for a daughter it would be that she treasure each day like it was the last one she would have. Life is full of wonderful people, beautiful places and interesting differences. I would want her to experience as much of life as possible—experiencing different cultures, tasting new foods, learning a language, talking with people.

If I had a dream for a daughter, it would be that someday she could experience the amazement of having a child. Then, one day she would understand why I look at my two boys the way I do, why I love them for making me laugh each day and why I thank God each evening for putting them in my life.

Kristi Shoemaker

With one of the brightest smiles I know, Kristi shares her energy with bank marketing, her community and her family.

Past

When I was a little girl, my great-grandmother would tell me stories. Stories about when she marched for women's rights. Stories about when she got pregnant even though she wasn't married and the disgrace it brought to her family. Stories about her disastrous first marriage and the scandalous divorce that followed.

Even though I was young, I understood that world. It was a world where women were second-class citizens. Yes, I knew that world very well—my father was king of our particular castle.

My great-grandmother died in 1978 when I was 21. To this day, she has been the greatest influence of my life. She instilled in me the passion to help other women. We must help ourselves, for we cannot depend upon anyone else to help us.

Present

In 1982, I started a job that changed my life. It was a low-paying, low-level administrative position. Luckily for me, this job—for the first time in my life—put me in contact with women who graduated from college. I saw women who didn't have to be married to be happy and successful women who led their own lives and were proud of them, and women who knew what it meant to be a mentor! What an epiphany for me. All the stories that my great-grandmother told me were beginning to make sense. This is what she fought for—the right of women to do and be whatever they wanted. I wanted that freedom!

The year I turned 30 was the turning point in my life. I divorced my husband, I quit my job, I moved to Cincinnati and I began college full-time. I was finally able to realize my dream. I had wanted to go to college all my life and now I was going. But, soon, the doubts began to set in. Was I smart enough? Was I too old? Could I really do this without a man to help me? The answer to all of those questions was a resounding YES! I was smart enough. I wasn't too old and I really could do this without anyone's help. Every day I could feel my great-grandmother on my shoulder encouraging me, telling me I could do it!

A couple of years went by and I met a wonderful man and got married. When I was only

15 credit hours from graduation, my husband lost his job. So, in 1990 I left my dreams behind and quit college. I started work—once again in a low-level, low-paying job—and then I started my own company in my spare time. A short time later my company started doing so well that I quit my full-time job.

By 1999, my husband and I had built a comfortable life, but there was always something missing for me. So, after much encouragement from my husband, I closed my company and went back to college. I graduated in one semester and in August 1999 started working on my Master's degree. In a year and one-half I will begin my Ph.D. program.

Working on my Master's degree, I do a lot of research on women's issues—the suffrage movement, the 1960s and the seemingly backward spin that the women of today are falling into. Many of my female peers—even though only in their 20s—think that the glass ceiling has been shattered, sexual discrimination is a thing of the past, and that the ERA is just around the corner. I feel like my great-grandmother when I tell them stories of how I fought to be recognized and respected.

Future

Things are much different now than during my great-grandmother's day. And, it's much easier for women who are entering today's workforce than when the women of my generation began working. But, ladies, we still have a long way to go! It is our responsibility to push forward, to break new ground and mentor the women of tomorrow.

My dreams for our daughters are these: May you one day be judged and paid by your work performance and not by your gender. May you one day tell your children about the day the ERA was passed. May you one day encourage your daughter to pursue her Ph.D. in any field she chooses. And, may you one day look back and tell your granddaughter about the time you had to decide which of two women candidates to vote for as president!

Deborah Spangler

Deborah is the president of Deborah Spangler Communications with offices in Cincinnati and Indianapolis—and she loves antiques!

Dear Little Granddaughter,

How fun it would be to sit down and talk to you over a cup of tea or a lemonade! I want you to know the many ways in which my life has been a joyful one—and how much I hope that you, too, will find happiness in yours. Here are a few tips from your grandmother:

First, cherish your family. Be good to your parents and love and keep close to your siblings. I hope that when you are young you will develop some rich and lasting friendships. What fun it is to share memories with those who knew you in your growing years! As you get older, keep in touch with them—a letter, a birthday card—celebrate with each other. But always be ready for new friends in your life. We women truly need each other; and as we age, new friendships widen our vision and offer us loving support.

Take good care of yourself—physically, mentally and spiritually. Learn to enjoy your own company when you must spend time alone. Have some hobbies, and read, read, read! Always try to keep an optimistic outlook on life—as they say, "look at the cup as being half full instead of half empty."

Stay interested in the world around you. Appreciate nature, even in very small ways. If you have time and means, travel and learn about other people—they are fascinating! Find a cause and work hard for it. Remember there will always be people who will need your skills, time and energy.

Try to do one kind thing each day for someone—call a lonely person, stop to chat with someone on your daily walk, write a letter, pay someone a compliment—just any small gesture that will give someone a moment of pleasure. And at the end of each day, thank God for the day you have just lived. And stay flexible!

Love, your grandmother

Elizabeth Peterson

"Betty" Peterson is a tiny person with a huge heart. Her determination that people be treated equitably, fairly and humanely is unequaled.

I am a mother-to-be and I couldn't be happier at the prospect of bringing new life into the world. Even before I received this opportunity to participate in this collection of dreams, I had given much thought to my prayers for my own child—my daughter. I wish for her all that my fellow sisters and I have struggled to achieve. I pray that my daughter and all of our daughters know themselves on the deepest level and can say and live out "I am."

- I Am Strong.

I am strong enough to walk away from harm. I am strong enough to say NO when something does not feel right. I am strong enough to face my emotions and life challenges with full conscious awareness.

- I Am Wise.

I am wise enough to know that I don't know everything. I am wise enough to take responsibility when the responsibility is mine. I am wise enough not to take responsibility when it does not belong to me.

- I Am Independent.

I am independent enough to walk away from anyone or any relationship that isn't good for me. I am independent enough to speak my mind and my truth without needing anyone to agree with me. I am independent enough to decide for myself what kind of life I want, what kind of work I do, and how I choose to experience God.

- I Am Worthy.

I am worthy enough to never have to prove my worth. I am worthy enough to be unaffected by those who do not and cannot understand me. I am worthy enough to live life according to my own vision.

- I Am Student.

I am a student in this world and ready to learn from all that happens to me, both wondrous and challenging. I am a student in this world and show respect to all those who have learned hard lessons. I am a student in this world and I learn from others who are still students themselves.

● I Am Teacher.

I am a teacher and I honor my own wisdom. I am a teacher and share with those who wish to learn from me. I am a teacher and my teaching rings out through the example of the life I choose to live.

● I Am Forgiveness.

I am forgiveness and forgive all those who do not know better. I am forgiveness and forgive those who know better and who are not strong enough to act better. I am forgiveness, and I forgive those who cannot find it in their hearts to forgive.

● I Am Quiet.

I am quiet enough in my own mind and thoughts to hear and experience that which cannot be described and that which is greater than I can imagine. I am quiet enough to experience the beauty in the smallest things. And I am quiet enough to feel joy in the sound of my own heart beating.

- I Am Gratitude.

I am grateful for all that I have and for all that I will have. I am grateful for all the simple things in life, which support and comfort me. I am grateful that I am part of a loving, abundant universe.

- I Am Proud.

I am too proud to allow someone else to dictate how I feel about myself. I am too proud to be arrogant. I am too proud to think of myself before others.

- I Am.

I am all that I choose to be. I am living my highest dream of myself. I am ever evolving. And so I AM. I AM. I AM.

Shira Block

A specialist in the field of human potential, Shira conducts workshops and seminars focusing on personal growth and development. She is the author of "Step-by-Step Miracles: The Handbook for Successful Living."

earn as much as you can about and from your mother—you may want to deny it, but you will become her one day!

Think freely. Think positive. Look for rainbows. Work hard. Laugh often. Take a chance. Try something new. Don't stand still. Make some mistakes—Learn from them. Believe in yourself.

Carol Duke

A dyed-in-the-wool Texan, Carol works for a major pharmaceutical company.

f I could create the world that my daughters would live in, to be able to give them the skills and the attitudes that would best serve them in the future, I would wish for them the following:

- Understand that you can do anything you want. You are as good as anyone else. You are a special combination of your mom and your dad, your grandma and grandpa and so many other people who have had an influence on you. You can climb mountains, or search for buried treasures, you can dance in a Broadway play or perform with the Royal Shakespeare Company; you can be a zookeeper or a veterinarian. There is no limit to what you can do—except your own imagination. Set your sights as high as you want them to go, and you will get there.

- You don't have to do everything. If you choose to take on smaller challenges or decide that life is special right here at home, that is wonderful. You can choose to be a scientist or a mother or both. The point is that you get to choose. And, whatever you choose, if you are happy, is OK.

- Have lots of women friends. They are the best source of comfort and joy. Make many and hold on to the very few who are special and will last a lifetime.

- Don't judge your value by what others do. There will always be people who have more and are ahead of you, just as there will be those who have less. Determine what you believe to be the best you can do and strive for it. Be happy with who and what you accomplish.

- It is said that you are as happy as you choose to be. Choose to be happy. Attitude alone determines whether we look outside and see bad weather or a rainbow. Every failure provides an opportunity—but, you have to be looking for it. The opportunities, the rainbows, the joy in life are there right in front of you just waiting to be seen. Open your eyes.

- Enjoy today. We spend so much time looking to the future that we miss what is right in front of us. Don't wish away your youth or any part of your life. Take each day as it comes and find something special in it. Life is a journey, not a destination.

There is so much more I want to say—take risks, take long walks, believe in God, exercise and take care of yourselves. But, now I'm sounding like a mother. The point is that you have opportunities and challenges and joys and tears awaiting you. My dreams for you are to be what you want and to be satisfied with that.

Kim Robak

A former lieutenant governor for the state of Nebraska, Kim Robak is an articulate speaker and a strong supporter of women.

My dream for our daughters, and everyone, is that someday we live in a world without hate and prejudice, where we are free to pursue our wildest dreams without discrimination or intolerance; a world where everyone is respected, treated fairly, and never abused; a world filled with helpfulness and harmony.

Charlene Marie

Stricken with Guillain Barre Syndrome at 21, Charlene became the first woman service technician for a gas company and joined the National Guard in Alaska. She has a home-based business where she grows, dries and wholesales grass and grains to west coast florists.

I am a family of women. I have no daughters. My mother, my sisters, my grandmothers, my friends are who I am. I lived almost one third of my life viewing the world through the skewed lens of feminists afraid. Afraid of becoming different, afraid of not becoming different. Pictures of my grandmothers when they were young bear no resemblance to them as older women. Their sparkle was dimmed by their flowered house dresses and their chunky shoes and their tightly curled hair. Although there was laughter, there was also a standard they were taught to adhere to that left no room for the giggles. To this day, I still feel guilty at times about the irreverence and irrelevance I feel toward matching silver and crystal, and always doing for others. My grandmothers, however, usually had the final word in the lives of their family. I recognized when I was very small that in my family, the women were the strength and substance. This was not talked about, of course, and the women like Eleanor Roosevelt were secretly admired, with some trepidation.

My sisters are now, finally, my friends. We share a history of striving toward excellence when we were young in a world that really only rewarded female habits of generations past. We share an instinct of strength. My sisters were excellent then and they are excellent now—with many battle scars to show for their efforts to understand that it was and is, really, really okay to become women who are not only stronger than many of the men in our lives, but have been called upon to demonstrate it numerous times.

My mother has been the source of my greatest strength and also my greatest regret. She did not expect to have daughters who read voraciously and who, at times, ridiculed her for her own choices. She did not expect to battle with them at every turn because they did not conform to what she thought was certainly true. I believe that it was her generation of mothers that had to accept the most changes in their idealistic view of their daughters, and then come to powerfully believe in the rights of all women. My mother, just like my grandmothers, is strength and substance. My mother also teaches me everyday to believe in the unseen and the unheard.

My friends are my gifts to myself. They are women who believe in me and who have shared their knowledge, experience and struggles without thoughts of conceit—or shame. We too share that thread that has been interwoven through the generations, "Do we have the right to be the best we can be?" And we have all answered, "Yes, we do. No matter what."

Every female in this world is a daughter. So for them, their grandmothers, their mothers, their sisters and their friends, I dream of a world where they are always striving overtly and with pride to become women like Eleanor Roosevelt, wearing the coolest clothes no matter what age they are, and using paper plates whenever they feel like it.

Karen Wamsley

A feminist at heart, Karen's talents are in her organization and efficiency—and her terrific sense of humor!

My dreams for my daughters are to face each day with respect for themselves and others. To go after their interests in life and strive to succeed even through life's struggles. And to love someone who will make them feel strong and important. And, of course, to be happy.

Lisa Wylemans

Lisa lives—and dreams—in the heart of Tennessee.

I have such dreams and feelings for our daughters. While I have not had any biological daughters, I have been fortunate enough in my lifetime to use my energies, commitment (and as I got older my understanding of "connected vision") with girls and women from all paths of experience and ages.

I quite by accident stumbled into this remarkable journey. I attended an all girl Catholic high school in Cincinnati, Ohio, a school that had remarkable, caring teachers. Teachers that spent time with bringing out the best in me. As well prepared as I was for the business world, my education lacked information as to what happens to girls in a culture consumed with diminishing women's voices and rights. Words like "rape," "dating violence," "choices," and "strength" were just some of the words missing that needed to be addressed. I never really felt a sense of connection with women in my past or my present.

The choices laid out in front of me were marriage, nursing and teaching. To deviate from this was costly. As a young woman I knew of girls that were harmed both physically and emotionally by those who said they cared for them. They suffered their pain in silence because there was no room in a society to bother with women's issues. Little by little I saw them disappear.

Through the years I have been involved with so many women victimized by rape, domestic and sexual violence. More and more I saw the continuation of what silence does to women—the disappearance continued. Keeping women isolated is one of the best ways to make sure that women keep shrinking. Not much seems to have changed since my days as that high school student.

What is my dream for our daughters? This is it: That they will invite the women of their past into their lives. That they will learn what great strength and wisdom comes from these voices. That they will never give up their right to be taken seriously. That when they say "No" they mean "No!!" That they will not allow anyone or anything to diminish their spirit for long. That they will see themselves as part of a long line of determined, courageous, visionary voices whose spirit, humor, guts and inner solitude forged the path for us today. That the accomplishments of Elizabeth Cady Stanton, Susan B. Anthony, Sojourner Truth, Barbara Jordan, and their mothers will be as familiar to them as Madonna and the other pop culture "icons" of the day.

One last thing I wish for our daughters—if and when the time comes that they have the opportunity to walk with their mothers in their last journey of life, they value every moment of the experience. We are our mother's daughters, and for so many of us, what a gift that is.

Be women of integrity—
Voices for the future...

Ann L. Hoschler

A spunky redhead who spends one weekend a month with women in prison, Ann is a former nun who works in the area of domestic violence.

It's difficult to go back fifty years+ and try to remember what hopes and dreams I may have had for that tiny human being we brought into the world, but I'll try...

My dream, my hope, my wish for our daughter was that she would always do her best in making her dreams come true, and always with courage, with passion, with humility, with a concern for others. And she's done that, and even with some of the tough "bumps" she's had to face, she managed to keep her wonderful sense of humor, her joy in living and in giving.

Helen Boosalis

This former mayor of Lincoln, Nebraska was a candidate in this country's only gubernatorial race with two women vying for the state's top elected official. Her opponent, Kay Orr, won in 1986. Helen's political advice continues to be sought, and she is active in AARP.

reams for our daughters—happiness and the ability to recognize the opportunities that are surrounding them. The courage and self-confidence to pursue their education and self development with gusto!

Hetty Jane Markin

Retired from the world of personnel recruiting where she owned her own business, Hetty Jane spends her time now traveling the country.

dream that when I die, my daughter Barb will still love me, for that will mean the family cycle of mother/daughter animosity will be broken.

I was forty years old before I could look into a mirror and not see someone ugly. Forty, before I could begin to silence the childhood criticisms that shaped my adult life. Forty, before I quit my childlike striving for my mother's acceptance, realizing I had to move on without it.

My parents' first child was male. In the process of trying for another son, mother gave birth to five daughters. She finally had another boy, the two of them almost dying in the process. The sons were favored, the five girls made to know they were somehow inferior.

My sisters and I grew up insecure and angry, scarred by our own mother's insults. We were ugly, we were fat, we couldn't do anything right. The men we dated and married were never acceptable, our achievements paled in comparison to our brothers', our choices were always wrong.

My mother's actions were a continuation of her troubled relationship with her own mother, and I have followed her lead into a stormy relationship with her. Attempts at reconciliation have failed. I carry forever the pain of having my mother tell me I wasn't wanted. I will always wonder what it's like to be a child wrapped in the arms of a warm and loving parent. Now and again, I will contemplate how different my life might have been...if. When my mother dies, my tears won't be for what I lost, they will be for what I never had.

It's one of life's ironies that my mother, who didn't want children, had seven, and that I, who wanted several, had one. I'm careful with my eight year-old daughter Barb. I want her to know that she is wanted and loved, that she is beautiful inside and out, that she is a wonderful and talented person.

I dream that my daughter will enter adulthood with more confidence than I did, and that her life's choices will not be drawn from a well of despair and negativity. I hope that I will have the grace to let her develop into a woman, guided and encouraged but not restrained. I dream that Barb will be saddened at my passing, yet thankful that I was her mother, and that if she has children, she will want and love them all.

Diane Walkowiak

Owner of her own business in public and motivational speaking, Diane is working on the restoration of an older home, successfully using barter to gain some of the goods and services she needs.

I often have friends or family ask me for tips on bolstering girls' self-esteem. Though working with girls is my profession, I often ask myself questions about the same thing! But, I have noticed a pattern.

The issue often surfaces after someone has seen a daughter, sister, niece, neighbor, or girl in their life succumb to some type of "esteem monster." Maybe they hate themselves for not making the team, feel like they should diet as a fourth grader, get excluded because they are gifted, or suffer from insomnia because they are worried about a test, a friend, or a family member.

Girls are hypervigilant, watching all the time, taking in everything around them. At some point, this internalization manifests itself, but it may seem to others that a meltdown is appearing "out of the blue." The tendency is for people—especially women—to want to solve the problem right away. *"Is there a program? A project? What can I do for her?"* The good news is that there are a lot of outstanding programs and projects (many listed throughout this book). The bad news is that programs and projects are only part of the solution.

In all of my studies, field experiences, and personal journeys, I have found that role-modeling, self-esteem and a healthy lifestyle are essential first steps to encourage girls. That means not only talking to a girl about it, but living it! Pep talks will make little headway if the pep-talker isn't practicing what she preaches. I always remember the story of a colleague who facilitated an overnight retreat for girls where the theme was "Balanced Life." At one point she said, "No matter how crazy things get, you should always try to make the time to rest properly and eat well." Hours after the talk, the group shuffled off to the dining hall to eat and throughout the meal this woman needed to keep leaving the table to attend to various things like setting up for another speaker, confirming the bus pick up, organizing recreations, etc. One of the young women came up to her and quietly said, "I just want to remind you. *'No matter how crazy things get, you should always try to make the time to rest properly and eat well.'*"

Sharing expertise is another important, natural tool that women can give back to girls. There's no need to start a Girl Scout troop of one's own. As women, we can simply share our passions with girls—from web surfing to windsurfing. An artist called me once worried about her niece who didn't have enough to do. She thought her niece was in need of some fun, positive and educational activities. The girl resisted joining special groups or programs and instead wanted to hang out with her friends and liked spending time with her aunt, the artist. I asked, "Have you thought of doing some art projects with her?" She responded that she had, but felt that she wasn't much of a teacher and didn't have the skills to properly educate and motivate her. I told her that the connection to her was the best education she could give. She didn't need to have a teaching degree or be a youth minister to share knowledge and be a good role model.

I have found that in general, girls—like most of us—are interested in real connections with women and other people. The best programs constantly try to form these connections, but what really works best is when you don't have to try too hard.

My dream is that girls learn at an early age how gifted and vital they are, and also how to keep that alive as they travel through adolescence to adulthood.

Amy Kramer Brenengen

Amy's job is full of hope as she works with women to attain economic self-sufficiency. Fortunately for them, she is chock full of determination and creativity.

First and foremost my dream is that America can really be color-blind and that in the future it will not matter what color your skin is, or what shape your eyes are.

My dream for America is that women will have an unrestricted opportunity to serve in positions of power and authority without regard to gender in the board rooms of our largest corporations and in our most influential organizations.

My dream for our daughters is that in their lifetime they will elect a woman as President of the United States who will create a more just and equal society.

My dream for our daughters is that they will grow up and realize that there will be many less fortunate than they are and that they will be generous and giving in all ways personal and political so that all may enjoy the blessings of this land.

My dream for our daughters is that they will have the joy of engagement in political activity and fulfill their constitutional responsibility to help create a more perfect union.

My dream for our daughters is that this nation will have invested enough of its resources so that we will have removed the dread diseases of our lifetime through research and investigations in all forms of health care and medicine to remove pain and anxiety from diseases like cancer and AIDS, Alzheimer's, diabetes, and the like.

My dream for our daughters is that they will enjoy a national universal health care system which provides all who need care, access to the best there is.

My dream for our daughters is that the 13,000 children who now die each year from guns and violence will be a statistic of the past, and that their lives will be safe and that they will be able to walk the streets of America in safety without fear of rape or violence.

My dream for our daughters is that they will realize a life in America where abuse and violence in the home is no longer tolerated for them, for their children, or for their parents.

My dream for our daughters is that sexual harassment in the work place will be totally outlawed and that employers will see their responsibility to harbor a safe and secure environment for all their workers.

My dream for our daughters is that they be able to raise their families in prosperity, and that if they choose to work outside the home, their compensation be based on the true value of their work and based on equity.

My dream for our daughters is that their children enjoy the fullest of educational opportunity and that our national policy will be enlarged and enhanced so that higher education can be made more affordable.

My dream for our daughters is that they will grow old without having to worry about their health care costs and becoming a burden on their children or on the community.

Finally, my dream for our daughters is that they will never have to see the day when their loved ones have to be sent off to war and that throughout their lives there will be peace and tranquility.

These are my dreams for our daughters.

Patsy T. Mink

Patsy Mink is a member of the United States House of Representatives representing the Second District of Hawaii.

F or my future daughter:

I hope…

…that your eyes will always shine with the happiness of knowing that you are loved,

…that you will laugh freely and often,

…that you will radiate with self-confidence,

…and that I will be as good a Mom to you as mine was to me.

I wish for you great, life-long friends, true love, and the capacity to face whatever you may encounter; I wish for you success, in whatever terms you choose to define it, and I wish for you to know how very much I love you.

Joy Williams

This wonderful woman with the bright smile and the good heart hails from the South, where women of substance are known as "Steel Magnolias"—and she is one.

One of the greatest lessons of my life was learned when I was fourteen. It came with the opportunity to ride on a bike trip to a small, remote ghost town—just like you may remember from old TV westerns. This town was about 65 miles away from my home, down a busy two-lane highway.

After much parental discussion (yes, my friend's twenty-something year old sister was chaperoning), it was agreed that I could go. Training for the big weekend meant riding my blue stingray (with the banana seat) around the neighborhood for a couple of days. I had no idea what I was in for and borrowed a friend's three-speed for the occasion.

Saturday morning, the group I was to ride with met at the State Capitol. I had my poncho, my hip-hugger bell bottoms, and my black three-speed! As we began the ride out of town, I experimented with the bike's gears. We'd just picked it up that morning and it was my first time on any speed bike. I was a bit horrified when I realized the bike was broken and it wasn't going to move out of first gear!

I was tired before we got out of town. I knew I was in big trouble. After four hours on the road, we stopped for lunch. I thought I was going to die and I still had 40 miles to go. Each hill seemed like a mountain and I would almost cry when I'd have to ascend another. A couple of times I literally begged the follow-up man, Duane, that if I could ride in his van the rest of the way, it would be so much better! He was very convincing when he told me that I was doing fine and I could make it on my own the rest of the way.

Well, I did make it. Sunburned and tired, but I made it! What exhilaration and delight I experienced that evening. I have to admit the worst part about being there was imagining the trip back. We were riding a different way and adding about ten miles to the trip. How would I make it home?

Sunday morning was overcast with a threat of rain and much cooler than the day before. Riding felt better than on Saturday; everything was easier—at least it was before I wiped out on a steep hill going in for lunch. So here I was—tired, aching, injured—and then the rain started pouring down. I was more miserable at this point than at any other point in my entire life. I wanted to be warm, I wanted to be home, and I still had forty-plus miles to go.

Do you remember the song by Simon and Garfunkel, "Cecilia?" That was the rhythm I found to pedal to. For forty miles, I sang, "Cecilia, you're breaking my heart, you're shaking my confidence daily. Whoa, Cecilia, I'm down on my knees, I'm begging you please to come home…"

You know what? I stuck it out. My determination pulled me through; I made it home.

Life for me is no different than many others in having had many challenges similar to what I experienced that weekend in May, 1971. Several times I've wanted to quit rather than face what seemed an uphill battle.

My dream for our daughters is that you learn to find your own strength inside to carry you through whatever challenges that will arise in your life, and the difficult decisions you will have to make. And, if everything else fails, remember to sing in your loudest voice possible, "Whoa, Cecilia…!" and just keep moving forward.

Carol Settell Chappelle

With her family, Carol owns and operates a printing company. She is one of the most good-natured women I know, and gives unselfishly to her community.

DREAMS FOR OUR DAUGHTERS

I live in a rural area in the North East of Scotland—Moray. I have three daughters—Diane, 28, Pam 25 and Alison 24. One is married and expecting her first child, one is about to be married in three weeks time and one remains at home with me. There is no prospect of her getting married in the foreseeable future.

Over the last five years my world has been turned upside down—four years ago my husband walked out and has since divorced me and remarried, hence the reason I am back at college as a mature student and I am studying social science.

In short my dream for my daughters would be happiness, after the sadness that I have recently experienced. However in the real world I suppose happiness comes only in short, ethereal bursts and therefore should be grabbed whenever possible.

My realistic dreams for my daughters would be for them to achieve their goals in life whether they decide to be career women or mothers at home with children and husbands.

Rural areas do not always provide facilities which make it easy for women to either follow their careers or to be mothers who can provide all the experiences necessary for young children to develop and be stretched educationally and physically. In the future I hope that this will be remedied by better creche and nursery provision, good educational prospects and sporting facilities within rural areas thus giving rural inhabitants opportunities equal to those provided for inhabitants in urban areas, thus helping all women to achieve their life's work.

Andrina Taylor

Andrina lives in the countryside of Scotland where she is attending college and pursuing her dream.

My daughters, daughters-in-law, and granddaughters, for you I have dreams of JOY!!! This JOY comes from inside you—nothing outside can make it or break it. Happiness comes from outside and is made or broken by other people or circumstances. I have this JOY and I know that you do, also. Recognize and nurture it!!!

I dream for you Divine Order in your lives, that you be able to "Let Go and Let God." These two dreams will enable you to give and to receive love.

With dreams come rules for living happy, productive lives: As your daddy always taught you, "It's not what you make, but what you spend that counts in the long run."

- Spend less than you make. Give to church. Save regularly.

- Have only ONE credit card, and pay it off in full each month. (Forget the instant gratification bit.)

- Pay interest ONLY on house and car mortgages. (All else, save first, then pay cash.)

- IMPORTANT: have a DEPENDABLE car. (Looks and luxury are expendable.)

- Buy a GOOD mattress. (The bed and other furniture can be cheap.)

- Buy GOOD underwear and shoes. (All outerwear can be cute and cheap.)

- Invest in GOOD toilet tissue and facial tissue. (All other paper goods cheap.)

- Always be honest and trustworthy.

- To HAVE friends, BE a friend.

- Choose a husband carefully, one that you'd want to grow old beside.

My dear daughters, these may not really sound like "dreams," but they are my "goals" that I try to live by and pray that you will, also. Be loving and full of JOY!!!

God bless from Mama, Sue and Muzzy (Sue Fisher, Mama of Laurie and Peggy, Sue to Martha and Jennifer, and Muzzy to Capri and Laura)

Sue Fisher is a bundle of energy who, after a career as a teacher, began a new one as a realtor.

Thank God for the 60s! Women have a *few* choices now, especially in regard to their bodies and birth control. That in itself has given freedom to women, the freedom to choose! I dream of a future where my daughters can have choices in a safe and peaceful world, allowing them to follow their dreams.

Kristy L. Nerud

Kristy is in real estate, and has a reputation for her honesty and "telling it like it is."

elieve that we are all one people, all members of the human race. As children of one God, we are all sisters and brothers, relatives as the Native Americans teach us.

To hold the same standards for ourselves as we hold for others is universal in the major religions of the world, THE GOLDEN RULE. It places squarely on each of us the responsibility for our own conduct.

Hinduism "Good people proceed while considering that what is best for others is best for themselves." —*Hitopadesa*

Judaism "And thou shalt love thy neighbor as thyself." —*Leviticus 19:18*

Zorastrianism "Whatever is disagreeable to yourself do not do unto others." —*Shayast-na-Shayast 13:29*

Christianity "In everything, do to others what you would have them do to you, for this sums up the Law and the Prophets."—*St. Matthew, 7:12, New International Version*

Buddhism "Hurt not others with that which pains yourself."—*Buddha Udanavarga 5:18*

Confucianism "What you do not want done to yourself, do not do to others."—*Confucius Analects, 15:23*

Islamism "No one of you is a believer until he loves for his brother what he loves for himself." —*Mohammed: Traditions*

We can make this a better world if we go beyond knowing the words and begin to live by them.

Grab opportunities to meet people of other cultures in your community and around the world. Appreciate the heritage of each and see the big picture of your role in the universe. Be intentional about what you do and say.

Remember that human rights belong to each of us, equally, universally and forever. Including education, health care, adequate nutrition, and economic security among them.

Study the lives of people who have stood for rights of all and be strengthened by the knowledge that their ideas have been triumphant even though they paid a price for their stand.

Surround yourself with thinking people and work to act together for solutions to chronic barriers and make them bridges instead.

Know who you are and whose you are!!

Always work for a healthy planet with justice for all!!!

Shalom!

Marjorie Manglitz

Marj is a one-woman dynamo that has been a champion of human rights for over forty years. She is active in the United Nations Association and actively pressed members of the Congress for payment of back dues to the United Nations. She has made several trips to Mexico to work with native people to improve their economic status.

I t is my personal belief that each of us will be held accountable for how we have lived our lives according to God's laws. My primary role in this life has been as a wife and mother. When I am called before Gitchee Manitou, I will be asked how well I have lived that role and not how much money I earned or what titles I may have held.

Our children will do what we tell them to do, simply because they are our children. The testimony of what type of mother I was to my children will be in what values _they_ teach to my grandchildren.

My dream for my daughter and her daughter is that they will always be proud of who they are and where they come from. My daughter's beliefs in the traditions of her people are strong. I know that she will teach her daughter everything she has learned from her grandmother and I.

My dream for my daughter is that she will always be the gentle spirit that she is right now.

DREAMS FOR OUR DAUGHTERS

My dream for my granddaughter is that she will grow to be as strong a woman as her mother, with as much love and respect for others as her mother has shown.

Darlene Smart-Herrera
(Bad River Chippewa)

Darlene lives in an adobe house and warmly shares her American Indian culture. She mentors several young women and ensures that diversity is a part of everything in which she is involved.

As I sit and contemplate what I could dream for our daughters I am reminded that there is no better way to let our daughters dream than to tell them stories about our pasts and our mothers' pasts. I have no children of my own but am convinced that my mother was able to share with her daughters ideas, dreams, hopes and disappointments of her life and was able to pass down those lessons onto us not only to share with our daughters but all of those around us.

There are many lessons my mother was able to share with me; however, I am reminded of four of the more important ones which have helped me in recent years. I hope these lessons I have learned will help others learn and dream.

Don't throw balls in the house.

I am sure every mother says this to every son they have but probably more rarely to their daughters. Growing up I was told that I was able to do anything I wanted and what I wanted was to "play ball with the boys." My parents always allowed me to do what I wanted. I was never told I couldn't do anything because of my gender and I am thankful for this encouragement.

As I venture into the world where there are many glass ceilings and obstacles to bypass and overcome, I am elated that I was given an opportunity to play sports and compete at a young age. Playing sports has not only helped me in the employment world, it has also helped me stay focused and fit as I go into my mid-life and beyond into my elder-life.

I know my mother was angry the day my ball hit one of my grandma's plates sitting on the shelf, but I knew in the back of her mind she was saying...wow, what a great throw! Her only comment would have been, throw balls, just not in the house.

One day my mom came in the living room as my dad and I were debating the theory of gravity. He was trying to get me to understand all the principles of this theory when he picked up one of my mom's most prized crystal bowls and held it high over his head.

As we were discussing parts of the theory, including the speed at which it might fall to the ground, I looked at my mom. Her eyes were huge and had that look only a mom can produce. It's a look that you obtain when you have children. I am sure you acquire it somewhere around the third trimester and keep it with you forever. My dad had asked me the simple question, "What will happen if I drop this bowl?" Of course, he was expecting me to say all the principles behind the theory he had just taught me; instead, I said, "Mom will be really mad."

This lesson is something which shows me that we can teach our kids to use their minds as well as see what's outside the box. If we continue to expand our minds, learn about new things and challenge ourselves to be the best we can be, we will be able to see things others don't, or rather won't, see themselves.

Don't forget to vote.

Growing up in a political family I was often reminded just how important it was for us to be involved in government. My mother often told me how lucky I was that I was even able to have a voice and if I didn't vote I was just forfeiting my voice to the others who did vote.

I tried to use the argument, at times, that my vote didn't really matter until the one day after the polls had closed and the race between two gubernatorial candidates came down to the wire. One candidate, the one I had wanted to win, had lost by less than one hundred votes. This made me realize that if I had taken the time to make sure all my friends would have gone out and voted, then possibly the outcome might have been different.

Voting is the one way we as women can change the laws and policies which have been set by mostly men in past years. In order to dream and see into the future, we need to have a voice. We can do this if we would just vote.

What you sow is what you reap—ten fold.

My life has been changed forever because of the lesson that I learned as a young child. If you give to others, others will give back to you. My mom always made it a point to write thank-you's, little notes of encouragement and phone calls to people just to check in. Her ability to cut an article out of a newspaper and have it arrive in the mail just when you were thinking about that very topic was uncanny. Maybe it was the connection one has when they stay in touch with others.

Take time to volunteer and give as much as you can of your time and money to those who ask. You will not know what this really means to those lives whom you touch at the time but believe me, as I find old notes sitting around, newspaper articles I have filed or from the many friends my mom had touched over her years, I can truly say, I just know. When you give yourself to others, others will give.

The lesson.

I know that in order to dream we need to have a foundation from which to build upon. The lessons and collections that we learn along the way will help us have a strong base to grow, to act, and most of all, to dream.

Marcia L. White

Currently living in Utah, Marcia L. White is an avid golfer and has a keen engineer's mind. She has a knack of keeping projects on track and values good friendships...I am privileged to be one of those friends.

Who are our daughters? To me the meaning encompasses more than blood or legal relationships. I was so pleased and moved recently when a woman I'd guess to be in her 20s introduced me prior to a speech by saying, "This is Sarah Weddington. I had not met her before today, but I am her daughter-in-law." She was not referring to a legal relationship but rather to an inheritance of ideas, principles, and ideals. It is so important to me to have younger women who are interested in and who will work for the ideas and principles for which I have long worked.

I believe that when each of us thinks of dreams for the next generation, our initial thought is of memories of things in our lives that we wish had been different and the difficulties we experienced that we hope our daughters never know. One saying I like is attributed to Indira Ghandi: "I have felt like a bird born in too small a cage." My generation understood that and worked to push back the bars of laws, customs, and beliefs that bound women in too small a space.

As I was growing up, people often said, "Women don't... Women can't... Women shouldn't..." "They" said women couldn't work when pregnant. Today women can do so if they choose because we passed federal laws preventing discrimination based on pregnancy. "They" said it would be too strenuous for girls to play full-court basketball; my teammates and I were limited to half the basketball court. Today women not only play full-court basketball but also play in their own professional league. "They" said a woman's income couldn't be counted toward obtaining a mortgage because it was unreliable; she was likely to get pregnant and quit work, and her income would be lost. Today that also has been corrected. There are many "wrongs" that have been corrected through the determined work of feminists in the 1970s and 1980s building on the work of prior generations, such as the suffragettes. I hope younger women never experience those wrongs and that they will one day just be quaint stories of long ago. I do believe, however, that it is important for our daughters to know these stories so that they will passionately protect against going backwards.

When I was young, abortion in my home state of Texas was illegal except to save the life of the woman. It took the legal case of *Roe v. Wade* to overturn those laws across the country. Women now have a legal choice to continue the pregnancy and keep the resulting child, continue the pregnancy and place the resulting child for adoption, or terminate the pregnancy. But this legal right is being challenged by forces determined to make abortion illegal again. Access to abortion is being eroded across the nation. I hope that our daughters will work to ensure their legal right of choice and accessibility to safe, affordable medical services.

DREAMS FOR OUR DAUGHTERS

While we are glad that our daughters will "have it easier" and never personally experience what we went through, we worry that our daughters will lose a sense of where they've come from, not realizing how recently it was that women made these great strides that our daughters now enjoy. We worry that our daughters will take for granted these freedoms and fail to defend the victories of the past and extend them. I like the saying that "We stand taller because we stand on the shoulders of others." My generation was able to vote, for example, because of the work of prior generations. We've worked hard to expand the world of opportunities for women, and we need future generations to have a sense of place and history to continue that process of expanding opportunities. Each generation invests in the future of the next generation. I dream that our daughters will pick up where our progress has ended and carry the torch for generations to come.

Dreaming also brings to mind thoughts of what we would like to change immediately. I dream of a time when women will not be judged based on physical qualities, whether of thinness, sturdiness, or racial characteristics. It will be a wonderful day when factors beyond those are the important ones. I dream of a time when women will not be subjected to sexual harassment in the workplace, school, the military, or anywhere else. I hope that someday it simply will not exist. I dream of a time when there are so many female role models that women who achieve outstanding accomplishments aren't labeled "the first" and won't be exceptional, but rather the norm.

I dream of a time when government, businesses, men and women work together to resolve the often-conflicting obligations and demands of work and family, ultimately benefiting our entire society, especially our children. I want women to be able to more easily return to the workforce after being out for family obligations. The *Family Leave Act* was an important step, but there are many issues that it should and does not touch. I dream of a time when we don't have to continuously worry about protecting reproductive choices because those choices are assured, when we don't have to worry about each election and its impact on the preservation of the right to privacy concerning our bodies.

I have long dreamt of a time when there would be a wonderful museum devoted to women for people to visit. That dream will come to fruition on September 27, 2000, when The Women's Museum opens in Dallas, Texas. It is a project of the Foundation for Women's Resources, which I helped start and on whose board I sit. I want people to learn from its content, be inspired by the women represented, and look into the future.

I dream that our daughters will, above all else, be truly happy and find their niche. Our daughters have much more available to them than any prior generation of women has had. They are not frowned upon for pursuing the fields of math, science, law, or medicine. Technology is available to everyone, regardless of gender. I hope that they will embrace it and learn to love the computer. I want each of our daughters to discover what they love and have the courage to pursue it.

Faye Wattleton writes in her autobiography *Life on the Line,* "Your life's possibilities will expand or shrink in direct proportion to the strength of your courage." Daughters, do not be constrained by the voices of others. Find your voice. Listen to your voice. Use your voice to stand up for the issues about which you are most passionate as well as to stand up for yourself and your right to happiness.

To me, there's a third category of dreams, those we have for the world in general, a world that our daughters and sons share. We hope for a world of sustainable resources, of basic needs being fulfilled for all, of diverse peoples living in harmony, and a world of peace.

Sarah Weddington

In 1973, Sarah tackled the biggest case of her young legal career—that of defending the Supreme Court case of Roe v. Wade. One is struck by her serene nature and her staunch defense of a woman's right to choose. A native Texan, Sarah is actively promoting the Women's Museum currently being built in Dallas, Texas in association with the Smithsonian Institution (www.thewomensmuseum.org).

Keep learning, & learning, & learning, & learning, & THEN.... when you think you know quite ENOUGH. Keep learning some more!

Jeanne Baer

A national speaker and trainer, Jeanne helps people and companies do what they do best. Her professional approach and her casual presentations help people learn and grow.

I have put on paper a series of songs which have changed my life. For me, they are mind-body medicine prescribed by my awakening, stretching soul. The first poured out of my mouth in a continuous stream, leaving me bewildered yet greatly empowered. Before that day, I had not considered myself a songwriter. I still do not know how to write music.

I am a massage therapist, a bodyworker. I listen and use my hands to help people and other animals heal from physical, mental and emotional stresses, trauma and abuse. To date, my youngest client has been a twelve-week old child. To my knowledge, my youngest abuse client was three years of age. I dream for them. I dream that the wellspring of their inner wisdom will erupt and burst forth washing away their fears and lining their precious bodies with a loving resolve, tempered like steel yet warm as a smile.

I dream for the perpetrators, too. Victims creating victims. Some of them daughters of daughters. I dream that they will be lovingly guided as they let go of control and discover true empowerment. I dream that with an open heart, they experience tolerance and pass it generously down their family tree. I dream of peaceful hands joining in long, luxurious, sincere, gentle apologies.

Some of my clients have commented that I must lead a charmed life. "How do you do it—how do you stay so balanced?" I have been windblown to this light. I was bullied by bouts of depression, a dearth of coping skills and a fear of the truth of who I am. When I became engaged in my own healing process by people who truly listened, respected my needs and embraced my ideas, I floated on the wind instead of being tossed by it. I began to recognize life's opportunities. I have been windblown to a view of life which now includes regular doses of dreaming.

I believe we are all one, that we can see God in each and every face; so now, when I dream, pray or wish I ask for equal benefits for all. A dear friend taught me this generosity of spirit. I am reminded of it each time one of my clients is graced with the help of professionals who wade daily through a mire of social systems to create breathing space and peace of mind in lives filled with turmoil. I dream for these support people. I respect them. I ask they be granted not only money but enduring support systems of their own, opening doors to groundbreaking legislation. I envision days lined with truly unlimited possibilities to provide safe, healthy, long-term healing. I see them all smiling as the public comes to understand that helping one person lifts us all.

Like the rippling of water, influence is indeed far reaching. None of us goes in this world alone. I have let go of embarrassment to share about myself and watched eyes glimmer with hope. I am very grateful to those whose sharing empowered me. On most days, I sing out from a place in my soul which came alive in the moment when I dared to dream for myself. So, sing out from your soul, loud and strong, and ready yourself for a dream:

Clearing, clearing, clearing
I am clearing the past.
Clearing, clearing, clearing
the fear of a repeating of the past.
Clearing, clearing, clearing
Clear ringing of my truth
Releases, replaces the past.

Sherry Cole

This spiritual creature leaves a swath of serenity wherever she goes. She is currently sharing her gift of massage and healing touch in concert with psychologists working with young children who have been victims of abuse.

I dream that my daughter...

finds someone to share her life with

who ADORES her

for the beautiful person she is.

isn't held back by limitations or restrictions

and goes for it, achieving her objectives

 and making all

her dreams come true.

is BLESSED with good health;

realizes how fortunate she is,

as she is our darling daughter.

I dream that my daughter will one day have a daughter of her own and she will be her "rock" just as my daughter has been for me in those troubled times we have all been through.

I thank my daughter for being MY DAUGHTER.

God Bless ALL daughters, and sons, too!

Denise Apkarian Panattoni

Denise lives in England where she thoroughly enjoys being a mother.

y Dearest Jordan:

It's so hard to believe the year 2000 is here! When I was growing up, *The Jetsons* was one of my favorite cartoons. I always believed that the year 2000 would be very Jetson-ish. Now it's here and it's not quite as automated as the Jetsons was, but we are very close.

I was always the one from my clique who said I didn't want any kids. I'm a worrier by nature, and I could only think of all the things that being a parent would give me to worry about. Then one night (when I was in my late 20s and married to my second husband) I dreamt that I'd given birth to a beautiful daughter. I named her Ariana. I can't remember all the details, but I know that dream changed something deep in me. I discussed it with my (then) husband. We didn't quite agree on the type of motherhood I envisioned. (I wanted to be a stay-at-home mommy for at least the first year.) After our conversation, I knew that he would not be the father of my daughter. (Of course I would have a daughter!) He and I divorced not long after.

While your father and I were dating, I learned that he wanted at least one child, and that his cultural background was very supportive of full-time, at-home motherhood. Well, we decided to do the marriage and baby thing. Even though we planned you, when I suspected that I was pregnant in the early fall of 1996, I was afraid. I was so sick, at first I thought I had the flu, then I thought I was dying. I was ill almost all day, and tired all the time, too. We had been planning for months to move from my hometown of Washington, D.C. to Tucson, Arizona. When my pregnancy was confirmed, I don't remember even thinking twice about leaving all my family and going to live in a place where I didn't know anyone! What was I thinking?

To make a long story short, it was an adventure. I'd wanted to live in the Southwest for many years. I'd visited Albuquerque, New Mexico with a friend in the early 90s. Somehow, it wasn't for me. I'd visited Phoenix in the mid 90s with the previous husband. We'd driven down to Tucson, but it was dark when we got there, so we didn't see anything at all. So how did I decide to move to Tucson? I told your father about my desire to live in the Southwest. He said he didn't mind relocating. In the spring of 1996, I started Internet research and by early summer, I decided Tucson was the place to go. We decided that we'd move in the fall (after G-Ma's birthday). I had a premonition that I should start packing immediately, so I did. (Everyone thought I was crazy of course, but my hunch was correct. If I had waited, I would have been too sick to pack anything.)

My pregnancy, though marked with a life-threatening situation (for you) in the fifth month (surgery to repair a hernia that was causing pre-term labor), was a good one for me. I was lonely and sad a lot (new surroundings and no support system, you know), but I was so happy to be pregnant. I didn't really believe I was pregnant until I saw you on the first sonogram. It was so amazing. Instead of laying down like every baby I have ever seen in a sonogram, you were sitting up with your legs drawn up under you and your butt touching my womb. (You sit like that even now.) It looked so funny that I laughed out loud. You bounced up, then extended one of your little arms out like you were punching me. I really cracked up then. Your dad, the doctor and the technician all laughed, too. So you were special from the beginning.

DREAMS FOR OUR DAUGHTERS

As the months went by and you (and my tummy) grew bigger, you were the center of my life. Your dad worked at night, so often you were the only person I had to talk to. I talked, read, and sang to you all the time. In what was supposed to be my second-to-last week of pregnancy, I had gotten so uncomfortable, that sleep (and every-thing else) became very difficult. After two whole nights of no sleep (for you or I, it seemed), our midwife (thank you, Janet Nodine!) agreed to meet us at the hospital. We all agreed that it was time for you to make an appearance, and she induced my labor. You were born after about 19½ hours of labor. (It wasn't as bad as I thought, but the pain was a lot different than I'd imagined.) You were beautiful from the moment I saw you.

Well, even though your dad and I are no longer together, so far I've managed to achieve my most desired dream yet: being a stay-at-home mom. You are almost three now, and my wish is that my dreams for you will come to pass in the years as we grow up together.

Before I tell you some of the things I hope manifest themselves in your life, let me tell you some career advice that G-ma gave me when I was a teenager. She said, "If you learn how to type, you'll always have a job." So far, she's been right. I'm telling you that same thing, but I wonder how applicable it will be as you get older. I just finished reading Star Jones' book, *You Have to Stand for Something or You'll Fall for Anything.* Even though Ms. Jones planned early on to be an attorney, somewhere along the way, she learned how to type. She said that when she was in law school, it enabled her to be self-employed for more than the minimum wage that the work-study students were earning. Ms. Jones also went on to say that she's mechanically inclined, not needing anyone to change tires for her, etc. (even though she chooses to let others do those things for her—she's a true diva, you see). I'm just saying that acquiring many skills can come in handy in ways you never think about until you need those skills. (You have to read that book one day. Star Jones is a very fascinating woman. I've always enjoyed watching her on *The View*, but after reading her book, I have to say that I really admire her.)

I hope you will NEVER be afraid to do the things you really want to do. Even if you think the outcome may not be what you hope for, take the risk. Life is so short, and it can be such an adventure. It is always exciting and always new, but only if you choose to see it that way. I sincerely hope that your life will, in many ways, be more fulfilling and more exciting than mine has been thus far. I hope that by the time you are my age, you'll have achieved many of your wishes and dreams.

I hope that you will always aim to be accepting and tolerant of others' beliefs while standing firm in your own. The world has so much to offer: people of many diverse backgrounds who can share a multitude of experiences with you. Being accepting and tolerant will allow you to truly embrace others and learn from them, without fear of having your own identity swept into someone else's.

I hope that you will always remember that true happiness comes from within yourself, and not from some source outside yourself. If you are happy with your true self, you will be happy no matter what your surroundings seem to dictate. Always search within yourself when things seem to go wrong, and always be willing to admit when you are wrong. Your wisdom will come from being honest with yourself at all times about who and what you are. It ain't always easy, but it's always the right choice to make.

Never forget that you are a strong, capable, beautiful human being with endless potential. Using that potential in the correct way is always *your* choice. Make positive choices and you'll never wonder if you did the right thing.

Nam myoho renge kyo!

Love and happiness!

Mom
Richelle Roberts

Shelli lives in the East with her cherished Jordan. Her strength and determination are remarkable.

I have been feeling the difficulty of life these last few years so I have been reluctant to write something I would like my nieces to read. I want to be positive and uplifting for them. Life is hard enough. But they should know that. No one escapes unscathed.

When I turn to the positive, I have to admit that there has always been someone there for me. Always someone to offer comfort and support and sometimes guidance during the difficult times. I am not very religious but there is a Psalm I always turn to when I feel I've lost my way:

DREAMS FOR OUR DAUGHTERS

Oh my God you have searched me and you know me.
You lay your hand upon me.
Such knowledge is too wonderful for me.
Where can I go from your Spirit?
If I ascend to the heaven, you are there.
If I make my bed in hell, you are even there.
If I take the wings of the morning
and settle at the farthest limits of the sea
even there, Your right hand shall hold me fast.
If I say, "Surely the darkness shall cover me and the
light around me become night."
Even darkness is not dark to you
And the night is as bright as the day.
Search me, oh God, and know my heart
Test me and know my thoughts. —*Psalm 139*

The Rolling Stones put it more so my nieces
would relate:

You can't always get what you want

But if you try sometime

You just might find

You get what you need.

Love, Sara
Sara Christiansen, MD

Making her home in Virginia, Sara is a
compassionate physician who cherishes family.

107

To Nichole LaVon,

You are 19 at the time of this letter and you are a very savvy and lovable young lady. You have learned a few bad habits along the way as well.

You know I was born 3/56, graduated from high school 6/74, got married 7/74, and gave birth to your brother 9/74. Needless to say my senior year was quite a blur. I want to tell you I missed out on attending Barbizon School of Fashion and Rutgers University because of marriage and pregnancy. I want to tell you how proud I am that you didn't choose the same path.

I am glad I decided not to abort or put an unplanned baby up for adoption and once the maternal instincts kicked in, I wanted another baby. We always say we don't care if it's a boy or girl. But I truly wanted a daughter. Six years later, you were on your way to make a niche for yourself in the world. And I haven't regretted too many moments of your existence.

I am so thankful that you have so many choices and opportunities available to you. For me, it was…If you get pregnant…you get married, stand by your husband, take care of your home, work if possible, prepare the kids for adulthood, send grown children out to find their own places in life, retire at age 65, spend your retirement getting back to the marriage, bouncing and spoiling grandkids, and lastly you die.

Well, Nichole, "life happens." You are ejected into the world of reality and things just don't go according to plan. You and your brother are 19 and 25 years old now and are still living at home, people retire and they still have to work because social security is not enough to live on, and instead of spending this time with your spouse you have to plan your divorce. You relearn how to fend for yourself like you did before marriage. The dissolution of what you thought was forever is devastating to your mental self.

Well, without dwelling on what you are actually living, I think this has been an education that reinforces the old saying "Never put all your eggs in one basket." I put all of myself into others for so long, I have misplaced myself. There are bits and pieces of me inside of so many people and I didn't have any regrets until now.

Some of the things I wish for you with all my heart and soul...

...that you find someone that you can put your trust into and he/she makes you crazy stupid happy, like I was

...that you will continue to enjoy your own company and laugh at yourself

...that you travel, so you can enjoy home

...that you will be breast, uterine or any other typical female cancers free (the women in the family have been extremely lucky so far)

...that you will continue to share yourself and your thoughts with me

...that you will have the patience to accept others for what they can offer your soul and overlook age, handicaps and simpleness

...that you are your own best and loudest cheering section (I'll be second)

...that you have an abundance of friends. But if you have 2 or 3 best friends that will be all you need

...that you have lots of warm hearted moments, cozy robes, fuzzy slippers, hot bubble baths/showers, the vehicle of your choice, many champagne and roses dates, puppies at your feet, feelings of happiness, wrinkle free/no iron clothes, prosperity, endless success with your career as an auto specialist, insight to do the right thing (which may not be the popular thing), integrity

...that you are woman enough to face your consequences for your chosen actions

...that you have the strength to face, fight and win the war with any demons you may encounter

...that you continue to have the style to accept certain defeats and the ability to move on with grace

...that you have several "diamond and pearl" days

This isn't the last wish I have for you for the rest of my lifetime, only the last one for this letter.

...I wish you a few cloudy days and nights, so you can appreciate the sunshine of the next day.

I love you so much my precious daughter...

Mom, Naomi Landrum

P.S. And yes, I cried all the while writing this. <smile>

This wonderful woman types the most ebullient messages from the Midwest. She believes in the supportive nature of women and that we can all come together when it's for a great cause.

have a dream for our daughters....my dream is that there be unity, love and friendship amongst women of the future. I believe that women should stick together through thick and thin. We as women have a common bond. We are mothers, wives, sisters and daughters. We are known for our strength, love and wisdom. I pray that all women come together as one to share their love, strength and wisdom to make our world a better place.

Tonya K. Palma

Tonya—with beautiful cursive writing—has two sons and enjoys reading and walking...and dreaming.

s I look down at our daughter in my arms—her lips blue, and her body limp and seemingly lifeless, I ask my-self..."What would've I done differently if I'd known today was the last day of her little life?" Tears fill my eyes and I feel as though she and I are the only ones in the world as we ride in the back of the ambulance on the way to the hospital. We had been whisked away from the crowd at the graduation ceremony we attended only a few moments earlier.

We had been sitting near the back. The ceremony was only beginning when Emily, our twenty-month old, began making a rasping sound and jerking on my lap. I looked down and realized she wasn't just coughing, she was uncontrollably jerking, her body was stiff, and her eyes had rolled up into her head. My first instinct was to leave immediately. I carried her in my arms and headed out, pleading several times on the way out. "We need help! We need help! We need help!" As we made our way to the back door, a woman in the entryway took my arm and said, "I can help," and she began asking questions, assessing the situation. I asked her hopefully, "Are you a nurse?" She did not reply, but merely said, "Let's go outside." She ran to her car to get her cell phone and dialed 9-1-1. "We have a medical emergency," she said. "About 20 months old." She guessed accurately. Perhaps she was a mom, too. . ."Her lips are turning blue. She seems to have stopped jerking now. No, she's still conscious, yet anyway." Did they expect her to lose consciousness? She seemed so lifeless and unresponsive.

Although it had only been a couple of minutes, it seemed like an eternity. By now, a rescue worker was already on the scene. He was attending his daughter's graduation, seated about 20 rows ahead of us, when he heard the call and rushed outside to take her vitals.

Soon the ambulance arrived, and we were on our way. My husband and our three year old son were outside by now too and were preparing to meet us at the hospital. The rescue workers remarked on my incredible ability to remain calm. What they couldn't see was that I was trembling inside. I thought that somehow, if I tried to remain calm while I held and loved Emily, it might help—if only in some small way. Scary thoughts raced through my mind as I hugged and kissed her limp body, reminding her "Mommy loves you so much."

My aunt and uncle died in a plane crash several years before, leaving three small children behind. Since that time, it was not uncommon for me to get our affairs in order each time my husband and I took a trip—just in case we didn't return. However, in the ambulance I realized this was the reverse situation. I had never imagined losing a child—the thought was simply unbearable. Yet, as I pondered what I would have done differently had I known it was the last day of her precious little life, I felt at peace. I wouldn't have changed a thing. We had laughed and played hard earlier that day at the playground.

As a stay-at-home mom, I was able to enjoy our kids more in this short time than many moms do in a lifetime. I was certain of it, and I was truly thankful. Yet, I wasn't ready to lose her. I had so many dreams for her—dreams for both our children.

Emily was examined thoroughly in the emergency room and admitted for overnight observation. The doctors believed that since she had a fever when she was admitted, she experienced a febrile seizure—her body's way of reacting to a rapid increase in temperature. Although the doctors thought it might never happen again, it was scary to me, and I stayed awake most of the night watching her in that cold, sterile hospital crib, terrified that it might happen again. But it didn't, not that night anyway. That was nearly two years ago. Now, as she grows, I am thankful to

have the opportunity to share my dreams—
dreams for our daughter.

As I think of these dreams, I picture a rainbow with a heart at the end and a small cloud beside it. The cloud represents struggles, pain and conflict. If there were no challenges, the victories would be less sweet. Life is not predictable. The rainbow comes after the rain.

Ah, yes, the rainbow. In elementary school, we memorized the colors of the rainbow: red, orange, yellow, green, blue, indigo and violet. R-O-Y-G-B-I-V. And, that's how I've categorized my dreams.

R is for resiliency.	May you recover quickly from the challenges in life—drawing on your faith in God to sustain you during the difficult times.
O is for optimism.	May you look for the positive, or silver lining, in each situation. Nothing in life is all bad or all good for that matter, but try to remain realistic with a generally optimistic attitude. Be persistent. Stick to it; you CAN do it!

Y is for youthfulness.

May you maintain your youthful spirit throughout the years—singing, laughing and enjoying the little things. Continue asking questions, listening carefully, and being a life-long learner.

G is for generosity.

By giving of yourself, you will find your personal life satisfaction actually increases. Reading a book to a child, listening to a friend, or helping a neighbor recovering from an illness can be great "gifts." Be generous in your giving.

B is for beliefs.

May you grow to know who you truly are and what you believe in, so that when you are challenged, you have a firm foundation on which to stand. Learn to set specific measurable goals based on your beliefs.

I is for ingenuity.	Think creatively. Be original. Look at things from a different perspective. As difficult as it may be, embrace change, welcoming opportunities for personal growth.
V is for values.	Maintain high standards. Value life. Value people. That golden rule will come in handy—"Do unto others as you would have them do unto you." Think before you respond. Then, follow through on your word. Others will respect you.

At the end of this rainbow of resiliency, optimism, youthfulness, generosity, beliefs, ingenuity and values is a heart. The heart symbolizes love. In this sometimes cruel world, my greatest dream for you is to love and to be loved. With all my heart and all my soul, always know—I love you!

Amy L. Meisinger

Amy's dream...full of verbal color...arrived with a beautifully drawn rainbow at the bottom of the page.

When I was asked to write a story for *Dreams for Our Daughters,* I was very excited about the prospect because my daughter is so very precious to me; I want the world to be a safe place for her to live. Therefore, my goal is to use the opportunities I've been granted to make as much of a difference in the world as I can.

I strongly believe that every child deserves to be given the gift of health. This is the reason I support the work of the March of Dimes. For years they have made progress in research and education that helps mothers give their babies a healthy start in life. I am blessed to have two healthy children and I owe much of my gratitude to the March of Dimes volunteers and researchers who have made that possible. Though it breaks my heart to see unhealthy babies and children, I believe God doesn't make mistakes when it comes to children. They're all here for a reason. I hope that my daughter grows up to feel the same way. I'll certainly do my best to instill those values in her.

I realize that health education, especially for women, is not as accessible as it should be. As the Entertainment Industry Foundation's (EIF) Ambassador of Women's Health Issues and EIF's National Women's Cancer Research Alliance, my goal is to create an open dialogue amongst women regarding health issues so I can go to Congress and be proactive with the information. Not to do so, I feel would be a crime. I want my daughter to realize how fortunate she is to have proper healthcare and live in a country where healthcare is readily available. Women in other countries of the world and in areas throughout the United States are not so lucky. I'd like to use my website as a means for women to have access to healthcare information by providing them easy access to find information from experts. Perhaps by the time my daughter has grown up, health education will be easily accessible to everyone around the globe.

I want my daughter to have self-esteem that is unconditional. Not based on temporary things like looks or circumstance. I want her to take joy in the fact that God made her unique and special. I want her to know that God loves her in spite of any mistakes she will make. We all make mistakes, but when we have a sense of self-worth and value, our mistakes are not so self-destructive. I want her to be able to count on her parents for love and support, and to know that she is never alone, that God is always with her. I will pray that she chooses to follow the Lord. I will teach her about Jesus and his compassion for all people. I hope she will follow his teachings and learn not to judge people by the color of their skin, their size, their shape, or their ethnicity. I want my daughter to see people as they are on the inside, because I believe real beauty comes from within, and that's what's really important in our lifetimes. Physical beauty will fade.

I don't want my daughter to have preconceived notions of fame. I want her to be strong and independent, and make her own judgments based on observing all that surrounds her. I want her to realize that fame is a blessing and a curse—you can make it into what you want it to be, but once created, it can take on a life of its own separate from who you are. For that reason, you have to be grounded and stand firm in your beliefs. I admire the way Jacqueline Kennedy Onassis raised her children, Caroline and John F. Kennedy Jr. Mrs. Onassis believed that raising your children well is the most important job a person could ever have.

Despite the horrible tragedies the Kennedy families have endured, Mrs. Onassis obviously did an amazing job raising her children with intelligence, grace and independent judgment. I could only hope to do the same and will try to follow in her footsteps.

Another shining example of a mother raising her daughters well is my own mother Barbara Ireland. She raised my sisters and me to embrace the very beliefs I pray my daughter, Lily, will share with her children. I have a great role model in my mom and I'm happy to have the opportunity to teach my children the same as she taught me.

Kathy Ireland

Kathy Ireland is a lifestyle designer whose brand was acknowledged by Women's Wear Daily as the 7th most popular in its category.

All daughters deserve to live a life where they are free to pursue their dreams without fear of repercussions, violence, or ill will.

All daughters deserve to have the world celebrate with them, and support them in all their
abilities, and their accomplishments.

I dream of a time when all daughters will
know through action and deed that they indeed
can achieve any and all of their dreams and
desires.

I dream of a time when all daughters know
that their sense of self truly comes from within,
without the waste of energy it takes to learn this
over time.

I dream of a time when our daughters repre-
sent us in proportion to the world female population in leadership positions, government
representation and business ownership.

Karen D. Dunning

A strong and resourceful woman, Karen Dunning has
owned several businesses and travels to China to
collect cloisonne. Her expertise lies in finding
smaller businesses, growing them to their maximum
potential and moving on to a new adventure. One of
her latest achievements was moving to California,
where she earned her Screen Actors Guild (SAG)
card and appeared as an extra on "Chicago Hope."

It would be wonderful if, from a very young age, we could teach our daughters about self empowerment. The choices women make early on greatly influence the path their lives will take.

I believe one of the most important decisions we will ever have to make is who our life mate will be. As a young girl I believed that the 'tough talking, macho, hard living' guys were the ideal choices as mates. They would be strong, take charge kinds of guys that would make a woman feel safe and secure and somehow more feminine.

What I learned about those kinds of guys was that they were often insensitive, selfish, unloving, abrasive and downright mean at times.

My mother had also made some bad choices in her life as had her mother. We all believed that if we loved these 'tough guys' enough they would come around to our way of thinking and feeling. The truth is, once you commit to these kinds of men, you lose sight of who you really are.

My mother found a wonderful man when I was five years old. He treated her with great respect and raised my brother and I as his own. Before mom died just a few short years ago, she told me what she had learned about relationships. She shared her guidelines for selecting a life mate. Her list was short but one I would like to see all women use in their own search...

Listen for the words "Please, Thank-you, I'm sorry and I love you." Without these words the relationship is void of respect and destined to fail.

The eyes are the windows to the soul, look into them often for love, truth and support. A mate who cannot look into your eyes is hiding from something and will bring deception and mistrust into the relationship.

Look for the guys who may be a little on the 'nerdy' side. They are the good fathers, sensitive lovers and faithful mates. The 'macho men' often fall short in all of these areas.

As women we all have a responsibility to our daughters to teach them what they should expect and what they should give in a relationship. The cycle of abuse will end only when we believe it should.

Tracie Foreman

An author and motivational speaker, Tracie Foreman shared thoughts about mothers in her book, "Mama Knows." She is currently at work on her second book about fathers.

I dream that our daughters will live their lives free of the disease of alcoholism. Our family lived a lie for decades. Our daughters spent years in mental anguish and sorrow. We pretended to be perfect and came home to a very imperfect home. After a major intervention in their father's life, we began the process of healing one by one, day by day. Each of us in our own way searched for the way out of the darkness we all shared.

As their mother I had become an enabler and a cheat. I could hide my feelings and the outrageous episodes in our home. My dream for our daughters is that their lives can be drug and alcohol free. May God grant them Peace.

M. C. Schultz

This woman's bravery and honesty are the foundation of her gentle nature.

Opportunities—Internal and External

y parents gave me a precious gift—the confidence that I could be anything I chose to be. My later experiences in graduate school (seminary) and confronting the politics of ministry very nearly took that gift away. I still have little hope for the survival of Feminist Christians in ministry, and continue to experience deep ambivalence as I explore the calling I feel to serve the people of God.

My personal ambivalence may never disappear, and I need to come to terms with that. I find lately that breadth of career experience matters more to me than having been in ministry for twenty years. And I will always remember with joy my feminist ordination service and the public commitment I made in that moment to ministry with abused women.

For me, pregnancy and birth were pivotal experiences. I was unprepared for the intensity of the love I felt, and still feel, for my daughters. I have made personal and professional sacrifices for their well-being, and for my own. As I'm sure many women will agree, my happiness is often inextricably tied to theirs. I am MOTHER.

My dreams for my two daughters focus on creating internal and external opportunities for their significant and God-given gifts. I want to make sure they have the ego-strength and perseverance to attain their personal goals, whether or not those goals change over the course of a lifetime. And secondly, I want to do my part to eradicate sexism, which has such a long life in our culture! I will confront any voices they hear that are not empowering, and fight the structures that still exist that would discount their gifts and abilities because they are not housed in male bodies!

In our small town of Peru, Nebraska, I do what I can to make my point of view known. As a member of the American Association of University Women, I will play a role in bringing the daylong workshop of "Girl Power" to the Girl Scouts and other girls in our community who so desperately need to hear honest and encouraging words regarding their body image, relationship and reproductive choices. I will continue to strive for open communication as my daughters enter adolescence, and encourage their friends to come to me as well with their fears and the ignorance of others.

To My Daughters

Wren, may you fly free, piloted by your dreams and unhindered by human-made scenery and structures, shrugging off the opinions of others that are not supportive of your gifts and fledgling skills.

Linden, may you stand tall and strong and focused on the "still, small" voice inside you which speaks volumes about the person you were created to be and what your true capabilities are.

My darlings, always strive to be the best Wren and the best Linden that you can be, giving back to the world, and to your own children, your unique gifts of love.

You will be remarkable women. I look forward to being your friend.

Love always,
your Mom
Jeri Gray-Reneberg

An ordained minister, Jeri's eloquence in words and generous spirit set her apart. She is gifted in helping abused women.

Our three daughters are adults now. They are professional women, busy with lives filled with work, study and play. But our girls cannot have children. After years of medical research and fertility programs, their doctors have determined that adoption is the only option left.

Since motherhood is a God-given gift, I dream of a future with small children for them. Two of the girls want to mother a child. This dream is becoming a reality after months and years of waiting, taking parenting classes and interviewing with adoption agencies.

I see our daughters and their husbands with children, families filled with love and joy. I see these children as normal, rowdy, curious, fun. Prayer can move mountains and bring young children into homes with love to share.

Martha Hicks

After meeting Martha through American Business Women's Association more than ten years ago, I knew I'd met a special woman. Her feisty spirit led her through a successful business career and challenges.

I have one precious, talented, loving daughter, Shelly, who is expecting our first grandchild very soon. What an exciting time for our family!

My dream for my daughter and my granddaughters—lead your life by following the combined philosophies of your Grandpa and Grandma Scrimsher. Your Grandpa Scrimsher lived every day by the Serenity Prayer. He didn't try to change his weaknesses. He accepted them and managed them. Using his strengths of religious faith, relationship and intelligence he became a treasured friend and confidant of many people. A copy of the Serenity Prayer hung in his home and also in the Grainton, Nebraska post office where he was Postmaster from 1950-1977.

God grant me the power to accept the things I cannot change, the courage to change the things that I can, and the wisdom to know the difference.

Take time to find out what things you love to do, what things you truly believe in and what things you want to change. Then commit yourself to doing those things with the same determination and energy that your Grandma Scrimsher did.

BONNIE ALLMON COFFEY

Your Grandma Scrimsher was 2 ½ when her mother died. Because her father was not able to care for her, friends took her in. She coped with the death of her mother and with manic depression later in life by refusing to give up. We included this poem in her memorial service because she always had it hanging where she could see it. It described her attitude toward life:

It Couldn't be Done

Somebody said that it couldn't be done
But she with a chuckle replied
That "maybe it couldn't," but she would be one
Who wouldn't say so till she'd tried.
So she buckled right in with the trace of a grin
On her face. If she worried she hid it
She started to sing as she tackled the thing
That couldn't be done, and she did it.
Somebody scoffed, "Oh, you'll never do that;
At least no one ever has done it,"
But she took off her coat and she took off her hat,
And the first thing we knew she'd begun it.
With a lift of her chin and a bit of a grin,
Without any doubting or quiddit,
She started to sing as she tackled the thing
That couldn't be done, and she did it.
There are thousands to tell you it cannot be done,
There are thousands to prophesy failure;
There are thousands to point out to you one by one,

The dangers that wait to assail you
But just buckle in with a bit of a grin,
Just take off your coat and go to it;
Just start in to sing as you tackle the thing
That "cannot be done," and you'll do it.

—Edgar A. Guest

Sue Munn

A former elementary teacher who now travels the globe conducting training, Sue was a pro at celebrating Women's History Month with her students.

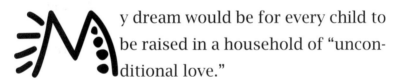

y dream would be for every child to be raised in a household of "unconditional love."

In our ever changing and fast-paced world, our daughters face the same challenges we do—and that is being treated equally in a man's world.

The girls who are raised with unconditional love will have the vital tool to deal with all life's challenges—that tool being high self-esteem.

Life will deliver the usual disappointments and sometimes difficult blows and my dream would be that the next generation of daughters knows when to take and to deal with their actions, but to know when the fault is not theirs and the responsibility lies not with them, but others who affect their lives.

Brenda Clements

A longtime friend, Brenda is a menswear buyer who is an avid spinner. Her strength is what amazes me, and her eternally optimistic attitude.

Dearest Maggie:

My friend is compiling a book of dreams for our daughters, so, naturally, being an opinionated and devoted mom, I have to include my dream for you, my one and only darling daughter. I'm so lucky to have been blessed with you, my dear girl. I truly believe you are a personal gift from God, especially for me. I hope you know I never take you for granted. Even on our "bad" days, I cherish and love you more than you could ever know. I have so many dreams for you—that you're always safe, happy and fulfilled. That you find your calling and follow your path, no one else's—the one that's just right for you.

My precious, I am your link to the past. You are my bridge to the future. You will carry forward everything that was started yesterday, and hundreds of years ago. You must never forget the significance of your obligation to womanhood and take nothing you have in your lifetime for granted.

You have the right to vote, not only in local bond elections, but your vote carries the responsibility of deciding who this country's next president will be. No vote goes uncounted. No vote is insignificant. Each vote has an individual stamp, like a fingerprint and sets in motion that which will be tomorrow. Women did not receive the right to vote until 1920. It was a long, hard, dangerous battle fought within families, in homes, streets and courts across our nation. People have grown apathetic and take voting for granted. Never let that be your plight. Vote with pride and conviction. Hold your head high and cast your ballot knowing you cast a vote for all the women who never had the chance to experience this simple, yet profound, privilege.

You can marry or stay single. You can have many children, or none. You can work outside the home, make your own money, own a business, property, stock, amass and retain your own wealth. No one can take from you what is rightfully yours. Our foremothers worked tirelessly so the women in today's society could be free. Not all women in the world enjoy these freedoms, but through your own hard work, clear focus and dedication, the world is yours for the taking. You can be anything you want to be my dear child. As I was growing up, my choices seemed to be wife, mother, secretary, teacher, nurse. Today you are not limited by any single person's, or society's, definition of what you should be or what is expected of you. You have the freedom to make your own choices. The list of "First Women Who..." grows shorter every day, but there are still battles to be waged and new grounds to conquer. Don't be fearful to add your name to that prestigious list. Never be afraid to be first—just don't stomp over anyone else to get there.

Get the best education you possibly can and remember, learning is a lifelong gift. We learn and grow every day. Some days I think I never really started learning until I turned 40. All of a sudden, it was as if I'd awakened from a deep sleep. I wanted to know everything, experience new things, tackle new challenges. I meandered through school, lost in a cloud of confusion. I had no direction, no goals, no mentors, no road map to help me along my journey. Listen to your inner voice, Maggie darling. It will tell you what to do and where you need to go. It signals your passions. Your gut will tell you when you're going the wrong way. These are your instincts—trust them. They will be true to you, if you only listen to what they're trying to tell you. Never be afraid to ask questions. Stand true and firm and make people listen to you. You have that right.

Seek out mentors. Use other people's lives as a map. If you were going to hop in the car and drive to Alaska, would you not ask others who've traveled the way before how they got there; what was the best route; what to be wary of? Of course you would. Life's the same. It's a journey. Ask questions.

Try not to let love get in the way of who you're supposed to be. This is so hard when you're young. Love becomes all consuming—your very reason for living. Finding a mate to share your life is the most wonderful adventure there is. However, too many women lose sight of their own personal goals when they marry. Maintaining a marriage is hard work—very hard work! Add to that running a household; then children. If marriage and children are your single goal, and you can accomplish that feat, so be it. Raising children is a job better left to the experts. Unfortunately, we receive more information on arithmetic than we do on human relationships. I don't use math every day, but I am a mom every day and motherhood has been the biggest challenge I've faced (thus far). Remember, a parent's main goal is to raise their young to be healthy, independent human beings capable of making a life of their own. You must prepare yourself for a life after they've grown. As time goes by, many women realize they've lost themselves somewhere along the way. (This is usually called a mid-life crisis!) Keep your focus and never forget you have a right to live your own life and fulfill your own dreams.

Understand that spirituality, just like your body and mind, grows over a lifetime. It's a long way from "Jesus Loves Me" to having a personal relationship with your God. It's an exciting journey, packed full of sweet surprises and remarkable personal insights. Don't neglect the trip—it's well worth it and just might be the most revealing of your life.

Friendship and fun. That is a joyful combination. Don't take life too seriously. Remember Mary Poppins said: "In every job that must be done, there is an element of fun." Someone else once said if you have five friends on which you can count, then, you have everything. I can attest to that fact. My friends mean everything to me, more precious than gold. There are new friends just waiting for you all through life. It's so exciting. Always keep and nurture your dearest, oldest friends. They add something to your life that nothing else can. Schedule fun times, plan trips, outings and adventures. Write letters, call often, stay in touch. Friends keep you grounded and add a very special spice to our lives.

When it's all said and done, among all the things I'll have done in my life, marrying your daddy and having you and your brother for my family, have brought me greater rewards and more immense happiness than I ever dreamed possible. I've been blessed and am forever grateful.

It's a wise saying: "No one plans to fail, but many fail to plan." When you look back over your life, will you be able to say, "Yes, it was interesting, exciting, fulfilling. I did everything I wanted to do and had fun along the way. I learned from the past, enjoyed the present, and planned for the future."

I wish for you the best and brightest life possible. I wish you love, laughter and longevity. I want everything good a mother wishes for a daughter. I want you to have it all—all in its proper time. I'll love you forever. Thanks for being my daughter.

Mom,
Cathy Wilken

Cathy and I are convinced that we were separated at birth. She is an author who collects anything connected with "Gone With the Wind."

've tried to think about what dream could affect any and all women, and I guess it is that little girls, no matter where in the world they are born, can live a life in which they feel totally safe, valued and loved.

Karen Heck

Karen lives in the East and offers a dream consistent with the theme of many of these special women.

ave I had dreams for my daughter?

Yes, I have had and do have dreams, and these dreams are saturated with hope and prayers.

Because her father and I are Christians, we had dreams of our daughter coming to an early acknowledgment of God and His love for her because those who "would draw near to God must believe that He is and that He is a reader of them that seek Him." (Hebrews 11:6 KJV) And as she would grow in His loving presence, we desired and hoped that she would also acknowledge Jesus Christ as her Lord and Savior, for then she would have His strength to rely on. These dreams and hopes have been fulfilled.

With the Lord Jesus as her Savior and shepherd, she can claim the 23rd Psalm for her own:

The Lord is my shepherd, I shall not want.
He maketh me to lie down in green pastures:
He leadeth me beside the still water.
He restoreth my soul;
He leadeth me in paths of righteousness for his name's sake.
Yea, though I walk through the valley of the shadow of death,
I will fear no evil;
For Thou art with me,
Thy rod and Thy staff they comfort me.
Thou preparest a table before me in the presence of mine enemies,
Thou anointest my head with oil
My cup runneth over.
Surely goodness and mercy shall follow me all the days of my life
and I will dwell in the house of the Lord forever.

—Psalm 23 KJV

Our daughter will always know she has a friend to love her and stand by her in whatever situation she finds herself. As she encounters trials, problems, troubles, as well as pleasant happenings and joys, we pray that she will remember and know that "neither death, nor life, nor angels, nor principalities, nor powers, nor things present, nor things to come, nor height, nor depth, nor any other creature, shall be able to separate (her) from the love of God, which is in Christ Jesus our Lord." (Romans 8:38, 39 LJV).

She has already faced situations that could have overwhelmed her and she faced them with loving kindness and courage as well as with fear and trembling. Our dreams for her have already materialized, for she is a happy, well-adjusted wife, mother, and grandmother as well as being a career woman.

I know that our dreams will continue to unfold, maybe down a different path than we would have anticipated, but as she makes decisions, that they will be good ones.

Now, we keep dreaming with hopes as we have a teen-aged granddaughter, a daughter-in-law and sons and grandsons and great grandsons!!

Jean Frederick

My great aunt Jean is what is known as "a good woman." Her benevolent nature and deep, abiding faith are truly something to know.

My dream for our daughters is that they are able to find and experience true passion in all aspects of their lives: passion for their work, for their friends, for their community, for their hobbies/interests. My dream is that they are born believing that this is their due, **not** that only the lucky ones find their passions, and that they continue this journey throughout their lives.

So many of us settle for less in our relationships and in our lives. And we wake up one day feeling incomplete and asking why. And we begin our search, wondering what we've missed along the way.

Life's fulfillment and joy is all about what we give and whom we touch. When we immerse ourselves in our passions, the giving and the touching are spontaneous and selfless. My dream for our daughters is that they find their passions, enrich others' lives through this journey, and leave this legacy for their own daughters.

Leslie Inman

A former vice president of marketing at a major insurance firm, Leslie has moved to the east coast, where she will watch the waves and seek a new adventure. She is committed to making her community a better place.

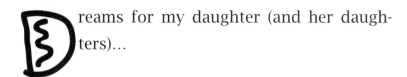

reams for my daughter (and her daughters)...

- that she and her daughters can walk alone and be safe

- that she and her daughters will be free to choose any occupation of their choice, and once in that occupation, will be allowed to create their space without limitations encountered because of their gender

- that she and her daughters will receive equal pay for equal work

- that she and her daughters will experience an education system that is dedicated to equal treatment of all students, regardless of gender

- that she and her daughters will experience an education system that is dedicated to the equal presentation of history, including the contributions of women and presenting them as equal in value to that of men

- that she and her daughters will experience media advertisements and media presentations that celebrate the bodies of women and emphasize healthy attributes, regardless of weight and shape

- that she and her daughters will benefit from medical research that addresses the special needs of women

- that she and her daughters will be free to control decisions concerning their own bodies

- that she and her daughters will respect the rights of others regardless of age, race, gender, nationality, religion, creed, or level of physical and mental capabilities

- that she and her daughters will understand that they must earn the respect of others

- that she and her daughters will exercise their duty to study the issues and candidates and to vote in all elections

- that she and her daughters will resist negative peer pressure and make positive choices based on their convictions

- that she and her daughters will challenge the stereotypes that they encounter

- that she and her daughters will understand that the peaks of life are the result of having been in the valley

- that she and her daughters will experience relationships that exalt in their

accomplishments and sympathize with their
disappointments

- that she and her daughters will hold dear to
  their hearts the family heirlooms and
  traditions that have helped shape their lives

- that she and her daughters will understand
  the value of hand-me-down clothes

- that she and her daughters will know the joy
  of sitting in the kitchen with a friend,
  sharing thoughts over a hot cup of coffee,
  chocolate or cider

- that she and her daughters will treat others
  as they would like to be treated themselves

Melba Cope

Melba is a pint-sized package of energy. She was
crowned Washington State's "World's Greatest
Granny" in 1999 and spent a year traveling the
country as "Granny Smith." Her passion is working
with issues of domestic violence and choice for
women.

My daughter Schy, nearly thirteen, is cool and confident in ways I still cannot quite grasp at almost forty. My dream for her is that she hangs onto that bounce in her step and cool confidence, that she can always see the wide selection of choices and never feel painted into a corner.

Schy spent from third grade in 1995 to sixth grade, December 1998 in a family that was focused on cancer; her brother, Levi, died at nine years of age of neuroblastoma.

She is amazing, considering how much she had to raise herself along and roll with the punches of uncertainty that a life-threatening disease brings to a family. Now she is so kind; her heart was broken wide to the underdogs, those struggling and suffering. She is a seeker of justice and a fountain of compassion.

I pray that she will always be blessed with the skill to turn pain into empathy and keep her graceful hand outreached to life, even knowing that sometimes, life bites.

"Without feather or branch, love brings us closer to the skies...we were part of paradise... once."   —*John Gorka*

Gail Lindekugel

This is one of those amazing stories that was discovered through the compilation of this book. To learn more about Levi and his legacy, visit www.lanefrost.com/laneslegacy.htm.

I dream that my daughter knows my love for her is unconditional and I will always be there for her. I pray that she will have a relationship with God that will nurture her spirit and give her a place of refuge. I want her to know in her heart and her mind that if she is willing to work hard she can be anything and achieve anything. I hope she understands the value of laughter and occasional silliness because they are the foundations of a happy life. I want her to remember that no matter how bad things seem today the sun will come up tomorrow. I want her to value her family and the amazing wealth of support and love her family has to offer. Of all my dreams for her, the most important dream is that my daughter will live her life and make decisions in a way that will reflect one essential truth—that she loves and respects herself.

Paige Roberts

An attorney who specializes in family law, Paige is now enjoying being a mom to her first child, Emma.

My husband, Steven Lee, and I are flying to Beijing on February 24 of this year to finalize the adoption of our daughter Joy Yan Dan Ping Hicks Lee. We will keep her native name, but have named her Joy—because it's short and sweet with all those other names (including my surname) and because it's our simple—or grand, depending on your point of view—wish for her life.

Joy was found alone outside the Nanping Welfare Home in Fujian Province on May 3. She is believed to have been born on April 15, but that's an educated guess by orphanage officials who have given her a temporary home—until we get there.

Joy is said to be among the favorites of the fifty children now living there. She's laughing, grabbing and sitting up. When we pick her up, she'll be ten months old. She'll be our first child and we've given her a great deal of thought.

Steve's dreams for Joy include teaching her to play golf—his passion since the age of five, something he did with his father and a sport that could help her as she goes through high school and college. Golf is a mental game, he says, and teaches discipline and perseverance—traits that could only help her navigate her life in South Texas, where the Chinese-American population is small. An award-winning journalist for a major newspaper based here, he also wants to teach her a love of words.

I'm a former journalist, now working in public affairs, and I, too, want to teach her the power and responsibility of words—including those in German and Chinese. I can say "I love you" in Chinese and I plan to say it often.

Among my other dreams: I want to pass on a life of reading and theater of the mind. I want to expose her, as our incomes allow, to the arts, the outdoors. I want her to know the preciousness of real friendship, which we've learned as we have experienced the lows—and now highs—of infertility.

Above all else, however, and as a woman who struggled with low self-esteem in my teens in the late 1970s, I want her to know her own worth. She's a completely wanted child. That, more than anything, will help her see life's vagaries as challenges and learning experiences—things to be embraced not feared.

Because Joy has two other biological parents, we can't guess what her strengths will be. Whatever they are, however, we plan to foster them. We want the 21st Century to be Joy's Century. And we'll do everything in our power to make that happen. We think it will be a joyous experience.

Lesli Hicks

Having known Lesli's mother, this dream brought wonderful news! Joy is a lucky little girl.

A Letter To Grandma Fern

January 2000

My Dearest Mama:

As I sit beside Susannah's bed, holding her little three year-old hand in mine while lullabies soothe her into sleep, I am overwhelmed by the love I feel for her and yet saddened once again at not having you, her Grandma Fern, my Mama, to share these precious days and to help guide her into her future. I understand now, Mom, what your knowing smile and gaze conveyed but your lips never uttered over all those years of my twenties and thirties: this "career" as a mom is every bit as important as the two-decade long managerial one I left behind when Susannah was born. This miracle baby, blessing Mark and me in our forties after three heartbreaking miscarriages, is growing up so very fast. She was fifteen months old when you died so unexpectedly, and she was just walking and beginning to talk. Now she is fully conversant and her curiosity knows no limits, challenging her daddy and me every day to explain life to her and to teach her what she needs to know.

DREAMS FOR OUR DAUGHTERS

Listening in the dark to her soft breathing, I contemplate Susannah's future, while reflecting upon the two generations of women who have preceded her. Your dream and destiny as a young girl was to marry well and to create a wonderful home for dad and for us as your children. You were such a tremendous success, Mama, raising two sons and a daughter in a beautiful and loving home, and maintaining a fifty-year marriage. I know, though, that you sometimes wondered what it would have been like to work outside your home.

As your youngest child and only daughter, my dream was to obtain a good education and to have my own career—just like my two older brothers and dad. This I did, with your encouragement and praise, by earning an MBA and moving to another city to pursue my career. In the process, I delayed marriage and children in favor of my job. I think I surprised even you when, after Susannah's long-awaited arrival, I chose to leave my hard-earned senior management position and move back to our hometown to be a "stay at home mom" and to get her closer to her extended family. In my own small way, I think I reinforced your life's work by my decision to stay at home full-time with our baby girl, and I cherish every minute that you and your granddaughter (and I) shared in the brief months after our return home.

Both of my "careers" have been tremendously demanding and rewarding, and I am thankful that I have been able to experience each. The fact that I experienced them sequentially rather than simul-taneously has given me interesting insights into each that I will pass on to my daughter so that she can plan her life as she wishes.

A big part of my dream for our precious Susannah is that she not feel that she has to choose between a career and a family to the extent that you and I did. I hope that she will find a world that can more readily facilitate both—without requiring her to be a "super mom" or to leave her young children in someone else's care. Even at three years old, I see an intellect in her and a drive to accomplish that should be nurtured and given an opportunity to contribute to our society. However, I would hate to see her have to trade her own baby's first steps or words for a corporate strategy meeting or to miss out on motherhood altogether without meaning to do so by trying to get her career well underway before beginning a family. While a career is tremendously satisfying, so is being the primary caregiver for a child the way only a mother or father can. I hope that Susannah can experience being a mom to the fullest and yet have a challenging career (if she wishes) when the time is right for her and for her family.

As I look at Susannah through the love of a mother's eyes, I realize that while I cannot pick the exact destinations of her life's journey, I can, as you did for me, help her pack for whatever the road ahead may bring. My dream for what she will take with her on her adventure includes much of what you wished for me and what I know you would want for your granddaughter:

- Enough love from friends, family and her life partner to last throughout her journey.

- Confidence in herself and her own abilities.

- Faith in a God who will be with her in good times and in bad.

- Dreams to guide her footsteps toward new destinations and, most importantly, the courage to always "Follow her Heart."

- Physical health and well-being.

- A strong education to prepare her for her trip and a lifelong hunger for learning.

- A childlike curiosity and sense of wonder about people and all of God's creations.

- An ability to find happiness in her world and to laugh from her heart.

- Honesty, a strong sense of her own values, and a respect for right and wrong.

- A world that is supportive of her life's ambitions—be it to pursue an active career, to be a wife and mother, or all three.

- The patience and good fortune, down the road, to find a man who will be her soul mate, lover and best friend, just as her daddy is mine. A commitment to "Hug each other tight and never let go."

- Lastly, may Susannah always carry with her the same type of friendship and unconditional love from me that I felt from you, and may she be blessed with a daughter or son whom she can love as deeply as I do her.

As I give Susannah a last stroke of her hair and a kiss for the night, I feel tears welling up within me—tears of thanks to God for blessing me with this baby girl and tears of gratitude mixed with sadness for having had you as a mother but not having you now. I go off to my own bed with an overwhelming sense of responsibility for the job I must do to prepare our little one for the world she will face as an adult. I will do it right, Mom, strengthened by the thought that you continue to smile down on us, but I sure wish you were here to help. I miss you so.

Your loving daughter,
Nancy

Through several telephone conversations, Nancy and I found ourselves to be kindred spirits. She put aside her professional career and now thoroughly enjoys playing hopscotch with her daughter.

I hope our daughters remember the many dedicated women who have worked so hard to give us the rights and liberties we all deserve.

My dream is that some day all women in our global society will be free from oppression and fear as well as valued because they are women. Wouldn't it be wonderful if some day our daughters could choose their life's work and have society accept their skills and abilities without legislation mandating it? That is my dream!

Future generations must not forget our struggle for equality and I hope our daughters will see history written to reflect these struggles and learn about the many "sheroes" that made our country the great nation it is today!

Pat Galitz

An instructor of business, Pat possesses the most infectious laugh. She is a good friend who has the capability to connect with anyone.

I wish for my daughters Michele, Beck and Lauren:

- A life that is filled with more peace than conflict

- A life that will include more laughter than tears

- A life with abundant love, rather than hate

My wish is they will never have to go through many of the trials and tribulations that I have, and yet I know if they do, they will become stronger, just as I had to.

My wish is they will never have to experience divorce, and all the hurt that is involved, but if they do, I hope they find happiness, just as I did.

I also wish that they find spiritual happiness, in whatever religion they choose. One day I hope they also will realize there is divine intervention and guidance, if you only listen hard enough.

I hope they are blessed with daughters, so they can also experience the immense range of experiences, emotions and all that being a mother involves. Each one is so unique, each one has taught me so many different aspects of motherhood, each one in her own way has contributed to my gray hair!

I hope they find the joy and miracle in giving birth as I did with each one of them.

I hope my daughters do not have to fight as hard to be recognized; I hope there is less discrimination in their lifetime and in their children's lifetimes.

Ultimately, I wish for them to follow their own dreams.

Cathy Maddox

Racing around in her tennis shoes and socks, Cathy is one of the brightest spirits I know. She and I became fast friends sharing a room at a national women's organization conference. She is a treasure with her delightful sense of humor and ever-present smile.

The things my mother always said are the things I hope to pass along to my daughters.

Remember, the three most important words are, "I love you."

Work hard at your job, you'll go far.

Always tell the truth; if you lie, you'll always be found out.

But the most important thing I found out from my mother...she was right!

Things I've learned...

Smile, giggle, try not to be in a bad mood, there are enough people in the world already who are, and if you run into one of these people, shower them with kindness, most of the time they respond with a smile. Never lose the child inside of you, let her come out and play once in a while.

Be empathetic.

Let the candle inside you burn brightly, never blow it out!

Pam Krafka

Pam's passion is anything to do with "The Wizard of Oz," with an entire room of the most fabulous Oz items.

ike many women, I had a stormy relationship with my mother from adolescence on.
We could disagree about anything and often did. I couldn't understand her and I was sure
she didn't understand me. I remember one night
in 1995, my brother called to say Mother was being taken to the hospital by ambulance and it did-
n't look good. It was that night I realized I wasn't
ready for her to die! We still had to figure out how
to be together! She didn't die then and soon I began taking little trips to Iowa to see her fairly regularly. We steadily began to build something,
although it wasn't perfect by any means, it was
better than we had ever done. There had been so
much to overcome and anything was progress. We
kept up our little healing visits for the next couple
of years.

Then, on Friday, August 22, 1997, I sat with
my mother at her kitchen table as we waited for
the time to come to drive her to the hospital for
colon cancer surgery. As we talked about all the
possible outcomes from convalescing at my house
to dying, she made me promise I would neither
allow, nor support any measures that were to
simply keep her alive. She talked freely about
being ready to die if that was the plan, and ready

to stay here on earth if "God wasn't done with" her yet. At 84, she was at peace with her life. And we had some peace and love between us.

On Saturday, September 20, 1997, I held vigil in my mother's hospital room alone. It was my weekend shift. All of us kids took turns being with her so she was never alone. A week after her colon cancer surgery, her internal stitches had slipped and her colon had dumped bile into her body causing a life-threatening infection. Mother had been in a coma off and on since August 28. Having been in some denial about what was happening, I was finally moved to ask the night nurse when she came in and was fussing with mother's IVs, "What is happening here?" The nurse looked at me in the eye and asked, "Do you want to know the truth?" "Yes," I said. The truth was that Mother was being kept alive without evidence, at her age and with the level of infection she had, that she could ever recover. The medication was just keeping the infection from getting worse and was not healing her. Mother was no longer eating (by her own choice) and the calories needed to assist her recovery, if recovery was possible, were monumental. They would have to insert a peg into her stomach to feed her and that was no guarantee that she would recover. This was exactly what my mother did not want.

I stood at my mother's side, held her hand and explained to her what was happening. She was the most alert she had been all weekend and looked at me with clear eyes as I asked her if she wanted the peg. She whispered no. I then asked her if she wanted the drugs she was being given. Again she whispered no. I asked if she wanted nutrition. No. Fluids? No. And then I asked the big question, "Do you want us to let you die?" "Yes."

At the moment my mother said yes, I began the process of saying my real goodbye. I later watched the doctor write "dc": on every medical order. I called one of my brothers and told him of Mother's decision and that I had implemented it. He said, "Good girl. That was the right decision." Even knowing that it was the right decision and that my brother supported me, my chest felt like it was being torn open and a fire of pain was burning inside me. My mother was going to die. And I was going to witness her death.

That night was the most powerful of my life and what happened there is what I wish for every daughter to experience. I looked into my mother's eyes and it was so clear that all that had ever mattered between us in my whole life was the love. NOTHING else had been real. All the past was wiped away except the feeling of love. I told her I would cry and she said, "That's okay." I needed to be physically close to her. The nurses kindly moved her toward one side of the bed so I could crawl up in bed with her. For the last time I physically laid in my mother's arms and yet for the first time, I laid there knowing the truth of our relationship. Love was real.

I do not have a daughter of my own but my dream for all women is that they will come to understand that all that has ever been real in their relationship with their mother is the love. Nothing else was true. I wish for them that they have that precious moment where they look into their mother's eyes and KNOW in their souls the feeling of love that passes between them and bonds them in an everlasting embrace.

Mary Kay Wood

Mary Kay's gift is that she helps people finds themselves again. She is a psychotherapist who frequently takes "Thelma and Louise" trips with her best friend to antique hunt the Midwest.

My dreams for my daughter include so many wishes. I want her to have good physical health and to be smart in prevention efforts—eating those veggies, exercising, not smoking or drinking alcohol in excess. I want her to have good mental/emotional health and to promote good health in her family by keeping life simple—not getting angry over small stuff, keeping a positive outlook, encouraging others, helping people in need and allowing other people to help her before she reaches a crisis point. I hope she obtains an education that enables her to choose a career that will utilize her gifts and talents while providing for her family. I sincerely hope that she uses great discernment while dating and waits to marry a genuine Christian man who loves her with all his heart. I hope she has beautiful, healthy children and that her dad and I can share in their raising. I dream that she will always live close by and we will see each other often. But above all these things, my ultimate dream for Jennie is spiritual—that her faith in God will carry her when any or all of my other dreams for her fail. So when the unthinkable happens—the cancer, the divorce, the accident, and all the other heartaches that life often brings when you least expect it—she will be strong in spirit and know throughout all these things that God is still in control and He cares for her. I pray that she becomes an example to her family and friends by the fruit of the Spirit—love, joy, peace, longsuffering, gentleness, goodness, faith, meekness and temperance (Galatians 5:22). My greatest dream is for her to teach her children and grandchildren to love and honor God and His teachings in the Bible so they will accept Jesus as their Savior and spread the Good News to others for this dream has eternal value.

Leslie Ward

Leslie and I shared great Southern food in the hills of Arkansas, catching lightning bugs, and putting them in jars when it got dark.

y dream for Avary*

My dream for you, sweet girl, lies not in the fairy dust of a wish, nor in the selfish fantasy of a desire, nor in the turbulent spring of a hope whose gossamer bubbles burst all too quickly as they come within our grasp.

Instead my dream for you comes in its truest and most real form, that of a prayer.

Dear God,

Please embrace my sweet daughter, my joy, my gift from you. Let her grow to know your love and feel her own potential through your love. Please cradle her heart so that she knows that by encompassing and radiating your love she will grow with peace in her heart and joy in her soul. Allow compassion for others to emanate from her very being so that they may be blessed and their lives enriched by her energetic, caring and wholehearted presence.

Protect her from the naysayers, those who would attempt to take even the last spark of confidence from her. If her heart seeks the complexities of formulas and chemical reactions, let her mentors offer her paths through biophysics as well as gourmet cooking. If her dreams weave through the universe, let none suggest realms other than space exploration. And, if her soul yearns to lead, then may no nation turn its back.

May she know that her desires and talents are not fleeting images but instead are gifts from You to nurture, protect and enhance for the good of those around her. Allow her to realize her highest and best purpose even as it transforms throughout her lifetime, allowing her to exult in the blessings of that purpose...be it lawyer, teacher, scientist, singer, president, nurse, minister or mother. Allow her the contentment of the moment and the peace of knowing that all that matters is being the conduit for Your love in each situation.

There are those who are happy in the complacency of their daily living. Those who have little or no time for the broken hearts around them let alone a moment for a meager gesture of humanity in the mere nod of a head or a warm greeting. I pray that she will never allow her heart to harden to any heart by refusing to see those on the desperate fringe of our society. Our world needs open eyes, keen ears and generous wallets. Please let her be giving in each aspect of her life.

Grant her the kindness and generosity of her grandmothers and may her heart beat as theirs, never closing to the point that she would presume to choose life's paths for others and never daring to impose her judgment upon those near her.

Surround her with Your love sweet God, hold her in your arms when she aches with sorrow. Lift her heart to learn from pain, so that she may rise to fly focused not on regret, dismay or anger but on the boundless beauty and grace of Your loving creation. Teach her that no wrong is to be harbored and that forgiveness heals, mending hearts and lives previously beyond human repair. Finally, let her know that she has a responsibility to use her gifts from You to the greatest extent possible, encouraging others with humor, healing lost souls with a kind touch and helping the wounded and weary with genuine compassion, wisdom and love. She will then know it is only by giving to others through Your love that she will attain the wealthiest of spirits and the truest contentment. Be with her God, let her cherish her family, savor her friends and learn to treasure your love beyond all understanding.

Amen.

Patty Pansing Brooks

*I pray this for my sons Taylor and Graham as well.

An attorney, Patty has been active in women's and civic issues. Today, she devotes time to her three children, all of whom have impeccable telephone manners.

My dream for my own dear daughter and for all girls of generations to come...is that each and every one of them will learn at a young age how important it is to LOVE yourself...body, mind and spirit. Whether it's soaking in a hot bath surrounded by candlelight, taking the time to nourish your skin with scented lotion, reading everything you can get your hands (and eyes) on, taking classes all through your life, or simply taking some quiet time to either experience glorious silence or listen to your favorite kind of music...we need to learn how to truly love ourselves before we can wholly and completely nurture others. The second wish I have for all daughters everywhere…is to have the wisdom and recognition that each day is a gift. You don't have to wait 'til you're older to express the gratitude for each precious day of life.

Cathy Blythe

As a radio morning show co-host and host of her own program, "Problems and Solutions," on KFOR in Nebraska, Cathy's sunny disposition is well-known.

In a perfect world, we wouldn't need dreams for our daughters. The young women we hold dear would walk with their heads held high, yet their feet would be firmly pressed into the ground. Needless to say, however, this is not a perfect world. In fact, it is far from it. I come into contact with this imperfection daily, constantly, as I'm sure you all do; but my contact seems much more tangible. I am a sixteen-year old that sees a very disturbing side to our nation's future; moreover, the people that inhabit it. Teens are growing up at an alarmingly fast rate. And before they can stop to realize this, they're grown.

For example: One of my friends had been hiding her pregnancy for six months. She was sixteen and completely terrified. My partner in English comes high to class every day. My neighbor received a minor in possession ticket two days before Christmas. The list goes on and on. The young people that I'm referring to aren't necessarily considered to be the "bad kids," either. They live in the high-class part of town, and their parents are well-known in the community. These kids are smart, their activities are just so blatantly common. It's important to state that my conscience is not spotless either; I, too, fit into the category of the above.

With that background, you can now more easily interpret the dreams I have for my future daughter(s). I truly believe the trait that would resolve the majority of teen problems is: SELF CONFIDENCE. I know the idea may sound commonplace and old, but I think these problems stem from a lack thereof.

I want my daughter to be a role model. I want other young women to look at my daughter and see something in her that they want in themselves. I want the comfort that she feels within her body, to radiate through her skin to be viewed by all. But, I want this confidence to exist whether she is a size 16 or a size 4, whether she is short or tall, whether she is handicapped or able-bodied. For when you have confidence, you can truly achieve anything.

Yes, indeed this world is not perfect, but beginning with dreams is a better place to start. At least we want something more than what we (or they) are getting. With a little help from God, hopefully all of the dreams I have for my daughter will come true, and if not, hopefully, the dreams she has for herself will come true.

Katherine Shea

Katherine continues to grow in Nebraska where she is active in athletics and with her group of friends. In the future, she plans to attend college and graduate with a journalism major and see where her life takes her.

DREAMS FOR OUR DAUGHTERS

Dearest Daughters:

I have so many dreams for you, too many to put on paper. First and foremost, I want you to be happy. Unfortunately, happiness can sometimes be difficult to find in this world, with its many ills. Just let me say that I dream that you live in a world unfettered from the things that seek to stop you from realizing your dreams. I dream you live in a world free of racism and white supremacy, sexism and male privilege, homophobia and heterosexism, religious and class discrimination.

I dream you understand there must be solidarity among women. Even if you don't agree with another woman's decisions, you must respect and allow her to make her own choices. I dream that you will understand that the right to exercise control over one's own body is inalienable, and you must respect it. I dream that you never allow privilege to get in the way of principle. I dream that you not let your relative status determine how you treat people. Do not allow your principles to be dictated or compromised by your privileges.

I dream that you will have a friend who loves, and likes, you just because you're you. People like that are hard to find, and if you have one friend, you will have experienced true love.

I dream that you will listen to your intuition when it tells you that what you are doing is right and/or wrong for you. Don't be afraid to follow your dreams; don't be afraid to fail; don't be afraid to try. Never forget that people have believed, fought, bled and died so that you might live free. Never be afraid to be, and/or apologize for being, the best.

My dream for you is that you live in a world that allows you to be.

Gretta Goodwin, Ph.D.

In 1998, Gretta was the first African-American woman to graduate from the University of Nebraska, Lincoln with a Ph.D. in Economics. She is currently working in Washington, D.C., and explains Keynesian economics so that even I can understand.

During times of industrial expansion and war women are a useful resource for employers. Politicians appeal to women to leave their sinks and join the workplace because "their country needs them." However, when it becomes politically inconvenient for women to work because of high unemployment, women are forced to return to the sink. To justify this policy, the government blames married women in the workplace for high unemployment.

Facilities that were provided to keep women in the workplace in boom times have now become a drain on the country's economy. They call this a time of recession. Women are once again called upon to help out. But this time, there is a reversal of policy, women are no longer needed. To help balance the budget, the politicians' solution is essential for women to take over welfare services as unpaid workers. The savings will be tremendous and women are expected to do this for the sake of the family and community at large. An alternative means of saving from spending on defense, sport, prison population, advertising and government propaganda exercises like consultancy fees, which are all largely men's occupational games, are not even considered. The spending on these unproductive areas cannot be justified against the everyday needs of the community, yet such expenditure is never questioned. Why? Because there are not enough women in the decision-making process to control unnecessary waste in the economy.

This is where we are today in Australia. The cutbacks in public services are presented as an economic necessity. The political campaign to promote the family is nothing but a covert policy to undermine the welfare state set up to keep women in the workplace and help the country out in boom time. Today, women are made to feel unemployment is their fault so they should get out of the workplace. Expensive social services will no longer be needed if women care for their children and elderly folk while men run the country, balance the books and create employment. Childcare, care of the elderly and education are the first to go, there are few voters in these groups. Once again, women will have done their duty if they answer the government's call to help the nation in this time of economic recession. Why must women always be the ones to make sacrifices? Is this ideology of women's self-sacrifice embedded in Christianity? Is this why so many women leave the Church?

The shift back to a Victorian concept of family threatens the sovereignty and rights of women as free citizens. It is a covert attack on the rights of women to be paid for the work they do and to be undervalued in the private sector as caregivers and community volunteers as well as their work in the traditional workplace. Most women in the paid workplace work a treble shift running the home, chauffeuring the kids as well as caring for elderly relatives.

This present government focus on family is linked to the media image of a community living in fear of rising juvenile crime, drug taking, youth suicide and growing dependency on the welfare state. The blame is placed largely on the breakdown of the family. By claiming things would improve if women stayed at home and looked after the children and elderly folk instead of neglecting their family duties, the solution rests with women. Fathers are not under the same pressure to take responsibility for these social problems; for them, it is business as usual.

The policy of closing down special schools, integrating disabled children into the school system and sending psychiatric patients out into the community with little support has added further pressure on families and community. On the surface these policies look acceptable, but who shoulders the burden? In the past, women fought for facilities to ease their burden of care; now, there is a danger that all positive advances in special care needs may be lost.

A media publicity campaign exposing the negative aspects of some corrupted institutions has justified the government closing down many excellent care facilities as well as the ones that needed to be closed down. This saved the government millions of dollars and also caused a great deal of community stress. White middle-class males, (WASPs), who make up the government and bureaucracy, accustomed to power, are now expressing their fear of the results of the feminist surge since the sixties.

Women's refuges were established to empower women who suffered domestic violence. Many women became empowered through educational opportunities in the seventies and eighties. They picked up the pieces, reassessed their situations in the light of feminism, asserted themselves and became successful in the workplace. Now, refuges and educational opportunities are being closed off to women. Lack of funding and increased fees in childcare and education make it impossible for single mothers.

The breakdown of marriage and traditional family life is blamed on working women. Men who decide to trade in a wife for a new model, just like his car, often walk away from his first family and expect to start afresh. What can a woman do in such circumstances today? She is labeled in derogatory terms as a single mother. Many object to her citizen's rights to support her children's health and education. Why should the children suffer? The law still favours men in divorce. A concept of responsible adulthood must be developed and taught to boys—to enable them to grow up to be responsible fathers who will share home duties as an accepted part of their life.

The Women's Liberation Movement empowered women to become political, to claim rights within the traditional family concept that historically excluded them as real citizens a hundred years ago. The twentieth century began well for women when they gained suffrage. Women don't want to start the twenty-first century fighting the same battles.

While we remember all the gains women made in the last 100 years, we must never forget how easily rights can be removed if women are not vigilant. Women and men should consider it an honour to be a feminist today. I am!

Mary Jenkins

Mary is the co-convenor of the Women's Electoral Lobby in Perth, Western Australia. She edits the Women's Electoral Lobby Broadsheet for women in Western Australia.

I have many dreams for my daughter, Xavier, but one in particular stands out amongst the other dreams..

Her beauty and grace is so astounding as I saw a vision of her while I slept soundly. I could see the sparkle in her eyes as she looked toward my presence. I spoke to her telling her how I loved and admired her excitement for life. I told her that she could do anything that she set out to do. Learn to ride that beautiful stallion called life. Ride it through the prairies but don't forget to exit at the big cities and the deep blue seas. You will ride across obstacles, but yet you will know how to untangle them and go on. Make sure that you also stop and see the less fortunate, for you have a lot to offer to them.

You are my dream that came true, as your dreams will also appear before your eyes while you travel. So ride my daughter, ride steadfast. Keep your head up along with the dust. Let that stallion runt and roar, you are what I am to live for. I dream more dreams as I will lay, but in my heart, you will always stay, Xavier. Xavier, my sweet dream, never forget that you are a human being, one who will shine along with the stars. So many people would like to be where you are. You will make them laugh and you may make them cry, but the only tears that you bring are the sweet tears that will dry up in their eyes. People will greet you and treat you with the utmost respect and you will thank them and give them your best.

So I say dream on and set your goals and never forget your dreams even when you get old, because hope and faith will lead you through anything that you set out to do.

I love you daughter.

Love,
Mommy
Julia Stubblefield

Julia is an artist who studied art and music in college. She is an articulate woman with a gentle spirit.

For my daughter, I dream for her a self-worth full of acceptance of being a female. I am very saddened to see the young girls in our culture selling out their femininity. As I was following a group of teenagers recently, both male and female, I noticed that it was almost impossible to tell one sex from the other. This was not just the way they were dressed (all the same), or the way they wore their hair (all the same), but also their physical mannerisms, the way they talk and the way they walk. I want my daughter to be proud of the fact that she is female.

I encourage her to have the strength NOT to dress like everyone else, ESPECIALLY THE BOYS. Just because a woman is feminine (and looks it) does not mean that she is weak or dependent. Women (young and old alike) can be both feminine and strong, feminine and independent, feminine and intelligent, feminine and assertive. So frequently girls are raised to believe that there is something wrong with looking the part. I see it as my job as a parent to remind both my son and my daughter that we can be proud of our differences and grow from them. Don't sell yourself short and don't ever believe that we are the weak or second best gender.

Looking the part is a small piece of being female. Maintaining that identity with pride is another piece. Believing in the equality of males and females is a dream I have for all our daughters. Over the last 40 years, our culture has seen a great deal of changes in regards to gender roles. I, personally, was raised in a family with very clearly defined gender roles. Even though my mother worked side by side with my father in the family newspaper business, she had the sole responsibility of all the household chores. This, after a

50-plus hour work week. After 35 years in the same house, my father still did not know where the dish towels were or how to run the washing machine. Needless to say, I made a different choice within my family and entered into an arrangement of 50/50 with my husband. In fact, immediately following my completion of graduate school and, needless to say, a very busy time for our entire family, my (at the time) five year old looked at me one night when I was making dinner and said, "Mom what are you doing in the kitchen? Dad cooks dinner." I knew then that my husband and I had provided for our children an example of a give and take, 50/50 relationship based on gender equality, not predetermined gender roles.

Diane Fern

A social worker at heart, Diane's passion is helping kids. She works with elementary and middle school children to help them hang onto their dreams.

For My Daughter

If I could give you
all the wisdom of the world
condensed into a charm

to wear around your neck

and whenever you

had any doubts or questions

you could touch

this pearl of life

and the answers would be

at your fingertips.

All the guidance, love

and knowledge

needed to ensure

your safe passage

in this sometimes

cruel and wicked world,

the compassion, wit and charm

to smooth rough edges,

all the faith you will need

to last you

until you get to

wherever you are going.

Oh, that I could give you

all of this—

a map of the path

through life.

But I will be here

when you need me.

You will have to find

your own path—

meeting your own obstacles,

creating your own solutions,

becoming your own person.

Charlene Neely

Charlene's poetry has appeared in "Songs for the Granddaughters" and "Plainsongs."

From daughter to daughter to daughter...

This special gathering of dreams is part of a family...the dream of my Mother, Dorothy Norris Allmon to her daughters, Rebecca Allmon and me, Bonnie Allmon Coffey; our dreams, and the dream of my daughter, Jennifer McLain Caffery. I thought it would be interesting to see the similarities, or differences in these dreams—all of which were written independently of seeing the others' thoughts.

id I, do I still, have dreams for my daughters?...You bet! I am truly blessed with two daughters. Even before their tiny, wrinkled bodies and new souls were first placed in my arms, dreams for them bombarded my brain.

As they grew and changed, so did their dreams...and mine. Some of their dreams were big to them at the time: A special doll for Christmas, a bike, a radio of their own, or just the right prom dress. Later...college money or a church wedding.

Too soon, my daughters stopped growing past the pencil marks on the door frame, and I realized they were "all grown up adults"...but my dreams for them kept growing and changing as they have.

I wish them to always be healthy and safe from harm. I wish them to always be truthful, compassionate, giving and to care about others. I wish them to always read, participate passionately in living, and never, ever lose their childhood curiosity and enthusiasm.

But most of all....I wish them to always know they are unconditionally loved. Because bank accounts, residences, cars, jobs, friends, lovers and some relationships come and go, but love hangs in there...and especially this Mother's love! I think a mother's love is akin to the whisper soft feel of a butterfly that touches your arm on a summer day, or the warm, snuggly comfort of a family handmade quilt when you feel lonely, or when it's just cold and rainy outside.

I know there are many mothers in the world who have dreams beyond their reach for their daughters. I also know there are many children born in the world, unwanted, who have no one to dream for them. This grieves me and fractures my heart, so what I must do, is try the best I can to make it better for them...and so must we all.

Mothers, daughters, sisters, grandmothers, aunts, cousins and all the male counterparts, have accomplished awe-inspiring dreams for daughters and sons. I cheer each one, because every child deserves someone to hold and cherish their dream.

Dorothy Norris Allmon

Known affectionately as "Red," my mother writes poetry and cooks five course meals for her friends.

The dreams I have for you, our daughters, is that you land your dream job.

Just what is a dream job? It's a job that you

- would do even if you didn't have to.
- feel important doing.
- cannot believe you get paid for.

- really enjoy doing.
- get excited about when you describe it to someone.

Warning: This is not easy.

I'm not going to tell you that getting your dream job is easy. It isn't! You'll have to spend a lot of time noticing, reading, asking and listening. You'll need (or need to create) a lot of self-discipline and patience. It's usually not an instant process. It may take years.

And even after you've found the dream job for you, the magic may disappear after awhile and you'll have to start all over again. (This is particularly true if you've been lucky enough to keep growing personally and professionally.) So, why bother?

Why torture yourself?

Look, most of us are not independently wealthy. We have to work for a living. Let's accept that and move on. But why torture yourself by working at a job you don't really like? Why not do something that absolutely jazzes you, and get paid for it? Life is a lot more fun when you're doing something you adore.

Which brings us to one of life's great secrets: work should be fun! I believe most people do not know or believe this. Perhaps even your parents either told you or showed you by example that work is NOT fun.

Most people don't think work should be fun because they either don't know how to find their dream job or don't want to work hard enough to find the right job for them. We all have choices. Make the right ones for you, and don't accept anything less!

OK, where do I start?

In case you're a little short on the description of your dream job, here are a few suggestions to help you uncover the dream job that is right for you.

Dream Job Recipe:

1. Notice what you did for "play" as a young child.

As a girl of 3, 6, and 9, what were some of your favorite playtime pastimes? You probably had several; did you have a favorite? What did your beautiful little head dream up for you to do and to be?

These childhood leanings can be ingredients for your dream job, if not the outright job themselves. Your natural innocence as a young girl may have prevented you from knowing enough about business to realize you wanted to be, say, a stockbroker. But your favorite made-up game of being a banker, or your love of the board game Monopoly, is a logical basis for a budding stockbroker.

One of my favorite things was to make up commercials for my mud pies. "Nutritious and delicious!" was part of my sales pitch. Some of my dream jobs turned out to be radio and television ad copywriter and "talent" (a misleading word!) for television commercials. Ultimately, I developed a love for persuasive communication. And I swear it all goes back to a 4-year old hawking mud pies!

2. Notice what fascinates you today.

When you surf the web, what sites do you like to visit? When you go into a bookstore, which section draws you in? If you have a zillion cable television stations available on your TV, which ones do you choose? When you read a newspaper, which section do you want to read first? Again, be aware of the topics that seem to have a magnetic attraction for you.

If "The Job" doesn't jump out at you, that's OK. Consider your interests to be parts of the dream job you want. Most jobs beyond basic assembly line work involve a variety of skills, so you'll need several.

"I'm not interested in anything."

You say there's no part of the bookstore that you like to visit? Don't really care about much of anything? Eek! Then you're probably bored and have a very dull, boring life. Ask yourself: is that what you really want?

Again, most of us will have to work for a living. So get busy and decide—make a conscious decision—to get interested in and be good at SOMETHING! I'm betting the interests are there; they're just buried deep under confusion or depression or low self-esteem. Decide you won't tolerate an excuse and get busy finding things you're passionate about.

"I'm really interested in X, but I could never find a JOB where I would get to do that"

Even if your interests seem odd to you, honor yourself by considering them real, not "just a silly thing." Consider talking with several people who know about the thing that fascinates you. Ask them what kinds of jobs exist for people with your interests. That's one way to seek out a "dream job" for you.

Yes, you may need to get more education, or have some on-the-job training to do that dream job, but it does exist! Ask questions of people who already have your Dream Job. What did they do before they did that? What kind of education did they need? How do they spend their day at work? Whom do they suggest you talk with to learn even more about it?

You think that job wouldn't pay enough? Don't give up! Keep asking around. "If I became very good at this job, how much could I make? You may not earn "the big money" right away (for the majority of us, it takes more than five years to earn that) but you'd be surprised what persistence and excellence can help you achieve.

Then again, how much money do you really need, if you were doing the job you really loved? Time to consider your priorities. How much do you value happiness and fulfillment?

"I'm going to be special!"

Decide (and you may already have) that you're going to be special, different, that you are going to make a difference. Keep that goal close to your heart; make it part of you and then...hold on!

Because believing that goal will take you places you never, ever thought you could go. Places you always wanted to be but didn't know how to achieve.

It happened to me and I know it can happen to you. Just believe in your dream and yourself!

Rebecca Allmon

Rebecca is one of the most resourceful women I know. She studies opportunities and researches information she needs to make good, sound decisions. She leads a purposeful life that is full of intent and thoughtfulness. She is my only sibling and sister.

y cherub Jenny…

First of all, thank you for the privilege of being your mother. I have not always been a good mom, and you and I have—separately and together—had some really tough times. I appreciate the opportunity to have come to this place of mutual love and respect, and to have watched you become the remarkable woman that you are. You are absolutely the best daughter a mom could hope for, and I am so very proud of your independent spirit, your dedicated love for what is right in the world, and your creative talents.

I wish I had a magic wand that could be waved to make all these wishes come true. Alas, the magic wand store has gone out of business. I wish for all daughters around the world what I wish for you, Jenny, and I wish that you…

…be strong enough to stay…in environments that are trying, in relationships that are developing, in situations that are demanding…

…be strong enough to leave…when relationships, environments and situations cause more pain than happiness, more degradation than is allowable and more compromise than is reasonable.

...support other women—we are, after all, sisters—some of us have lighter skin than others, some of us sing different lullabies, some of us wear different regalia...but we are all sisters.

...believe in and fight for choice in your life—and that you get the information you need to make the choices that are right for you and that you fight for the freedom of others to make their own choices—in their choice of work, in their choice of what happens to their bodies, in their choice of lifestyles.

...laugh—a lot.

...be open and tolerant and accepting. Embrace and learn from those who are different from you, because that's all they are—different, just as you are different to them.

...make time for yourself, to nurture your body and your soul.

...never take yourself too seriously...that you learn to find what gives your heart pleasure and—whatever it is—do it.

...find unconditional love, and have people who give you that love, while working on giving it to others.

...always remember the women upon whose shoulders you stand. Remember what they gave to you—the right to vote, the right to choose, the right to be an equal. Remember, too, that these rights are always being challenged, and it is your responsibility to ensure that those rights are never taken away from you. Be politically active, Jenny, because until we as a body of daughters are willing to activate our voting voices, we will forever be silent. Support qualified women candidates who support choice for women, both through your ballot and your wallet, as best you can. Even five dollars helps, and we have to start somewhere. NEVER give anyone the power to take away your freedom.

Know that you are loved and cherished—always,

Mom
Bonnie Allmon Coffey

An open letter from a future mother...

Right now, you are truly not much more than the hope in my heart and the wicked gleam in my husband's eyes.

At times, I consider the possibility that I may be unable to conceive or carry a child. I don't dwell on these thoughts but when they come up, I am easily comforted by the faith that one way or another, you and I belong together. It will never matter if I gave birth to you or received you as a selfless act of love from someone else. I have wanted you that much for that long. I love you already—the mere concept of you even before the conception.

I have dreamt dreams of you, dreams for you, ever since I can remember. Time has refined these dreams. I envision you more clearly now that I know your father. Not necessarily just your appearance, but the effect of the good man that he is. He is going to be a terrific dad. I have names, meaningful names, picked out for you. Until I hold your miracle of a body in my arms, your name will remain a secret teasing the tip of my tongue.

I will not lie to you. Life is not easy. I hope knowing that and knowing that I will always be your ally will make things easier. At the very core of our relationship I want your foundation to be unconditional love. I will never leave you. I will never love you for any reason other than just being you. I believe anything built on that can only get stronger.

The things that I want for you are not easily summed up. There are so many. My love, I want you to be full of hope and self-confidence. I want you to be a fair and compassionate person. I want you to have a belief system built on something good and loving and benevolent and forgiving—a guy we'd like to call God. I want you to have values, morals and ethics. I want you to be strong and that means strong enough to cry when you need to. I want you to be respectful, but mostly of yourself. I want you to be joyful and laugh easily and loudly and sincerely. I want your childhood to be about being a child and I want your transition into adulthood to be as painless as it can be. I want you to have a first love and a second love and a third. Please choose carefully. I want you to experience life a little before you settle down…it has so much to offer. And so, it would follow that I want more than anything to be the kind of mother to lead you down the right paths. I will always strive to be the kind of person I hope you can look up to and trust.

I don't know what the world will be like as you grow up. I will admit, I am not crazy about the one I live in. It isn't easy to gauge where things are going. I hope for a day when people are not judgmental of each other for anything other than their behavior and not how they love or the color they are or the God they believe in. I need you to know that hate is about fear and weakness and ignorance. I hope any stories you might hear of inequality, oppression or intolerance would seem completely foreign and something from the distant past. I would give anything if you never had a context for terms like "war," "terrorism," "animal cruelty," "child abuse," "rape," "murder," and a whole wealth of related topics. I pray for a world that becomes safer instead of spiraling down into violence and hopelessness. I promise to protect you the best that I can. I dream of your future with blue skies and green grass and trees. I hope that there is still pure organic food grown. I wonder if you will ever have to worry about diseases like AIDS, cancer and indifference. One of the most important things for you to know is that we are all sharing this planet and we are all in this together so we should make an effort to act like it.

You should know that nearly all relationships are complicated. I hope that your family is a haven for you. I hope that your father and I can be your very first and very best impression/experience of love. Our priorities will be our children and our marriage. If we slip away for a date or a trip, we hope that the lesson that you learn is that your parents are in love with each other and value their relationship. It does not mean that you are not fun to be around. It means that we believe that the marriage is the foundation of the family and it is hard to maintain one if the other is neglected. I dream of a love in your life quite so strong, sweet and fulfilling.

I can't even begin to express the excitement I feel when I consider you in the flesh. I have so much I want to teach you and so much to learn from you. I don't really have all the words that I want to say. We will both be learning as we go. Be patient with me. It is really important to me to get this right. I will close for now with one final thought...

My dreams for you are about your growth and well-being and happiness but in time you will begin to have dreams of your own. These are the dreams I wish for the most.

With all my heart,
your future mom.

Jenny McLain Caffery

Recently married, Jenny lives in Ohio where she continues to stand up for what is right, tries the latest recipes from her cookbook collection, and continues her lifelong learning.

About the Author

A native Texan and now an adoptive Nebraskan, Bonnie Coffey moved to Lincoln in 1989 to marry a high school mate who searched her out at their 20th high school reunion...see, dreams really do come true! Having lived around the U.S.A. and internationally, Bonnie is currently in her thirty-fifth home. She has excelled in twenty-six different work endeavors with fifteen different organizations. She has been featured in Kiplinger's *Personal Finance*, *Women in Business*, and "Strictly Working Women." She was named Nebraska's "Woman of the Year-2000" by Nebraska/Business and Professional Women, and has been honored by the YWCA and the University of Nebraska with their "Living the Dream" award. She has written monthly columns for two news publications.

She lives in Lincoln, Nebraska with her partner-in-life, Michael.

About the Artist

iz Shea-McCoy is a free-lance designer in Lincoln and has served as an Artist-in-Residence for the Nebraska Arts Council since 1991; she has also been a visual teaching artist in the Arts Are Basic program through the Hixson-Lied College of Fine and Performing Arts at the University of Nebraska-Lincoln since 1996. In addition, she has served as an art instructor in the Textiles, Clothing and Design Department at UN-L, the Art Department at Nebraska Wesleyan University as well as a mentor for highly gifted students in Visual Arts within the Lincoln Public Schools.

Liz earned both her Bachelor of Science Degree in Education and Masters Degree in Textiles, Clothing and Design from the University of Nebraska-Lincoln. She has been published and has won local, regional and national recognition for her work. Liz is currently communicating artistically primarily through collage and printmaking and is working on local commissions. Shea-McCoy has designed for retailers in Lincoln, Omaha and Vail, Colorado, as well as for manufacturers in Dallas, Santa Fe and High Point, NC.

DREAMS
FOR OUR
DAUGHTERS

incere thanks to the many women who shared their dreams...

Dorothy Allmon
Peg Armstrong
Jeanne Baer
Cathy Blythe
Phyllis Bratt
Amy Kramer Brenengen
Carol Settell Chappelle
Brenda Clements
Melba Cope
Christine P. Dodwell
Karen D. Dunning
Sue Fisher
Jean Frederick
Gretta Goodwin
Karen Heck
Martha Hicks
Kathleen Hurt
Nancy Intermill
Mary Jenkins
Caroline R. Jones
Naomi Landrum
Gail M. Lindekugel

Rebecca Allmon
Diane Deidre Bailey
Shira Block
Helen Boosalis
Pamela Bratton
Jenny McLain Caffery
Sara Christiansen
Sherry Cole
B.J. Dennis
Carol Duke
Diane Fern
Tracie Foreman
Pat Galitz
Jeri Gray-Reneberg
Lesli Hicks
Ann Hoschler
Leslie D. Inman
Kathy Ireland
Sandy Johnson
Pam Krafka
Karen Libman
Cathy Maddox

Marjorie Manglitz
Hetty Jane Markin
Amy L. Meisinger
Sue Munn
Charlene Neely
Marsha Ortiz
Denise Apkarian Panattoni
Elizabeth Peterson
Kim Robak
Richelle Roberts
DiAnna Schimek
Kristi Shoemaker
Cheryl P. Snyder
Julia Stubblefield
Brenda Vaccaro
Karen Wamsley
Sarah Weddington
Pippa White
Joy Williams
Nancy Wright

Charlene Marie
Sue McDaniel
Patsy L. Mink
Patty Murray
Kristy L. Nerud
Tonya Palma
Patty Pansing Brooks
Lois Poppe
Paige Roberts
Ina May Rouse
Katherine Shea
Darlene Smart-Herrera
Deborah Spangler
Andrina Taylor
Diane Walkowiak
Leslie Ward
Marcia L. White
Cathy Wilken
Mary Kay Wood
Lisa Wylemans

Girls today need dreams, and we as women need to continue to nudge those dreams along to reality. As you go through your life, you may be unaware that you are helping shape the dreams of a young woman.

If you have a dream you'd like to share, we'd like to hear it for our next collection of Dreams for Our Daughters.

Dreams for Our Daughters

www.dreamsforourdaughters.com
drems4dtrs@aol.com